Escape From Poverty:
28 Ways to Win at Life

Eddie D. Love, CPC

Copyright © 2015 Eddie D. Love

All rights reserved.

ISBN-10: 1515249247
ISBN-13: 978-1515249245

DEDICATION

This book is dedicated to my mother Maxine Hill and my grandmother Hattie Ruth Love. I thank you both for teaching me what it means to love unconditionally. I would also like to dedicate this book to my father, Rodrick K. Love. I know you are smiling down on me from heaven.

CONTENTS

	Acknowledgments	1
	Preface	2
	Introduction	7
	Early Life	22
1	GOD FIRST	57
2	I LOVE ME SOME ME	62
3	REPROGRAM YOUR MIND	68
4	CREATE A VISION	77
5	ACTIVATE FAITH	84
6	TRUST YOUR INTUITION	89
7	THE POWER OF POSITIVITY	97
8	FACE YOUR FEARS	104
9	JUST BE PATIENT	108
10	EDUCATE YOURSELF	114
11	SPREAD LOVE	119
12	FIND YOUR SOUL MATE	125
13	COMMUNICATION IS KEY	132
14	MENDING FENCES	137

CONTENTS

15	BUILD BETTER RELATIONSHIPS	141
16	UNDERSTANDING PERCEPTION	147
17	THE SIDE VIEW MIRROR	154
18	STOP MAKING EXCUSES	160
19	SHUT UP & LISTEN	165
20	PICK YOUR BATTLES	170
21	DON'T CONFORM	174
22	LIGHT UP THE ROOM	179
23	LEARN EVERY POSITION	185
24	OUT-WORK EVERYONE	189
25	ASKING BETTER QUESTIONS	194
26	TURN OFF THE TV	199
27	ASSETS AND LIABILITIES	204
28	GET PROMOTED	208
	Conclusion	214
	Notes	217

ACKNOWLEDGMENTS

First, I would like to thank God for his mercy and grace. I thank my loving wife Shapera for being supportive of all my aspirations. I thank my beautiful daughter Kylyn for inspiring me to be a better person. Thanks to my mom, dad, Shalundra, Darius, and the Knight family for the love and support. Thank you to my God-father Charles for the guidance over the years. A special thanks to my family; the Loves, Hills, Greenes, and Maggitts. To all my friends, thanks for the love and support. Lastly, thank you Tonya Tolson for editing this personal development masterpiece.

PREFACE

Growing up as a black male in America has its challenges but who doesn't face challenges in life? America is a place often referred to as the land of the free and the land of opportunity, yet there are homeless people roaming the streets in every town. Unemployment rates are at an all-time high. All this while the rich keep getting richer and the poor keep getting poorer and I know what the latter feels like. I've faced poverty in the Big City and the Deep South which of course had its differences. The one constant, no matter where I lived was family love and support. Honestly, if it wasn't for family members lending love and support, I'm not sure I would have survived. I need to give my humble thanks to each and every person that helped my family during our time of struggle. This book is merely one of the ways I have chosen to pay it forward. I want your children to read this book and pass it down to their kids. All my life I've been told that I wouldn't amount to anything but I have kept my eyes on the prize and I knew that poverty was the real enemy. Growing up in poverty, I knew I had to learn how to use my head and my hands if I was going to experience "The American Dream". I've since learned that the American dream is simply everyone's own fantasy and that you have to create the life you want for yourself. It doesn't matter how the story ended for others, you are the author of this one. I wrote this book to help you take control of your destiny and create the life of your dreams. I will use my personal story in this book and I will highlight the negative impact of poverty on society. These words will help you avoid experiencing poverty. I've learned that poverty doesn't care about race, religion, gender, location, sexual orientation, or political affiliation and you have to get your mind right or you'll be a victim of circumstances.

When I was a child I can remember people asking me, what do you want to be when you grow up? I really didn't know the answer to this question and depending on the day of the week you might get a different answer. I know I've said doctor before, just like I've said lawyer, and a few other professions that I didn't really know about. All I knew was those professions sure sounded good and I might have read that they make a lot of money. I always go back to the conversation that I had with my grandmother Hattie Ruth Love when I was 7 years old. I told her when I grew up I would be an entrepreneur. I still can't believe it happened and I also cannot begin to tell you what was going through my head because I couldn't spell the word entrepreneur. Since then, I've worked over 15 years in corporate America. I have held several positions such as Corporate Trainer, General Manager, Retail Sales Manager, Call Center Supervisor, Commercial Sales Consultant, Quality Assurance Analyst, and Process Improvement Specialist. My professional experience has had a major influence on my decision to write this book and I thank God for the positions I've been placed in. My personal life has also served as inspiration to write this book. I'm married to a wonderful woman and we have a beautiful child together. We also purchased our first home together in the city that brought us together, Charlotte, North Carolina. All these life experiences have shaped me to be the man I am today, despite the future others predicted. My ultimate goal in life has always been to help other people get what they want. Zig Ziglar is famous for saying, "If you help enough other people get what they want, you will get what you want". I've learned how to leverage my strengths in my everyday dealings with people whether personal or professional. I have taken my passion for helping and created the life of my dreams by becoming a Certified Professional Life Coach and author. As you turn the pages of Escape from Poverty: 28 Ways to Win at Life, I hope you are inspired to be a better person, help others, and achieve your full potential in life. You should view this book as a one month personal development program because I want you to read one chapter a day. Apply the **Chess Moves** at the end of each chapter to reinforce what you've learned each day.

INTRODUCTION

There's only one rule in life and that's learn how to play the game! I'm not referring to baseball, soccer, or basketball; however, you can make a pretty decent living if you make it to the pros! I'm talking about the game of life which I compare to the game of chess. All my life I've heard people say that chess is a thinking man's game. I've since learned how to play chess, and yes, I still suck at it! The important thing is that I understand how the game of chess works. Chess is a game that has been played for thousands of years and the object of the game is to defeat the other person by taking out the king. Checkmate occurs when the opponent's king is unable to escape from capture. When you really stop and think about it, chess is similar to life in many different ways. Your next move has to always be your best move. Each move has to be well thought out and you must think about the impact to the other pieces on your team. Another way to look at it is that you are represented by the king chess piece and everyone on the board must protect you. The chess board symbolizes the earth and the black and white spaces represent good and evil. The chess pieces symbolize the variations of people that you will encounter as you advance through the many phases in life. The single chess piece that I find the most intriguing is the queen. The queen can move in practically any direction and is the most powerful piece on the board. The creators of chess knew that a king needs a queen at his side if he's going to build a successful empire and win! Just like chess, winning at life is not an easy task but it can definitely be done in America. Unfortunately, in

America there is a huge disparity amongst the haves and the have not's. A small percentage of people have a great deal of wealth while a large percentage of people are facing poverty.

Take a look at these statistics on poverty, DeNavas-Walt, C. & B.D. Proctor. (2014). Income and Poverty in the United States: 2013, U.S. Census Bureau:

- In 2013, 45.3 million people (14.5 percent) were in poverty.
- In 2013, 26.4 million (13.6 percent) of people ages 18-64 were in poverty.
- In 2013, 14.7 million (19.9 percent) children under the age of 18 were in poverty.

- In 2013, 4.2 million (9.5 percent) seniors 65 and older were in poverty.
- In 2013, the overall poverty rate according to the Supplemental Poverty Measure is 15.5 percent, as compared with the official poverty rate of 14.5 percent.
- Under the Supplemental Poverty Measure, there are 48.7 million people living in poverty, nearly 3 million more than are represented by the official poverty measure (45 million)

How do we define and measure poverty in America today? Merriam Webster's dictionary defines poverty as, the state of one who lacks a usual or socially acceptable amount of money or material possessions. When I read this definition, it makes me wonder what the author means by a socially acceptable amount of money. Who determines what a socially acceptable amount of money is in America? Where I come from, I've never heard anyone say that they're trying to obtain a social acceptable amount of money. The other side to defining poverty in America is how it's measured. According to G.M.Fisher, The Development of the Orshansky Poverty Thresholds (2003), states: "There are two basic versions of the federal poverty measure: the poverty thresholds (which are the primary version) and the poverty guidelines. The Census Bureau issues the poverty thresholds, which are generally used for statistical purposes—for example, to estimate the number of people in poverty nationwide each year and classify them by type of residence, race, and other social, economic, and demographic characteristics. The Department of Health and Human Services issues the poverty guidelines for administrative purposes—for instance, to determine whether a person or family is eligible for assistance through various federal programs".

In America, cash is king and the enemy that I've had to face all my life has been poverty. Neither of my parents made a lot of money, so the reason we lacked financial resources is because they were underemployed or at times unemployed. We lived in poverty in Chicago, Georgia, and Mississippi and it has caused me to develop some very strong views about poverty, especially the impact it has on the African American community. Our household consisted of five people and my parents barely made 20,000 per year. The income amount fluctuated over the years because my parents spent several years apart over the course of their 25 year relationship. Poverty is not something that only affects African Americans but judging by the numbers, poverty affects people of all races the same way it affected my family. My mother was raised in a poor family with ten siblings in the Mississippi Delta during the 1960s. My father was also born in a poor family with thirteen siblings on the Southside of Chicago during the 1950s. This was during the height of the Great Migration for blacks in the United States. Many black people were traveling straight up the Mississippi river in search of better paying jobs and the "American Dream" It's hard to believe that black people were having so many children during these difficult times. From what I was told about my family, they had a lot of children so that the children could work and bring in additional income. By today's standards, it's common to see people with two children and they often gasp in amazement if you have more than 3 children. My wife and I often hear, "You have the little girl and now it's time for her to get a little brother to play with". We often laugh about this because although we make decent incomes, we want to make sure we can afford to expand our family with the combined and individual goals we have set. The poverty level for 2014 was set at $23,850 (total yearly income) for a family of four.

The chart below gives you the 2015 poverty guidelines broken down by family size.

2015 POVERTY GUIDELINES FOR THE 48 CONTIGUOUS STATES AND THE DISTRICT OF COLUMBIA

Persons in family/household	Poverty guideline
1	$11,770
2	15,930
3	20,090
4	24,250
5	28,410
6	32,570
7	36,730
8	40,890
For families/households with more than 8 persons, add $4,160 for each additional person.	

In all three places I lived in my early life, I witnessed a recurring theme, poverty. I witnessed a large amount of people working really hard to make a little bit of money. Growing up in the Deep South, just about everyone I knew was struggling to make ends meet, therefore I felt like my family's situation was normal. I was around 18 years old when I truly realized that I had lived in poverty my whole life. I knew we didn't have money for certain things and never owned a home, but I was oblivious about poverty. I had been familiar with the term but never really knew how much went into defining poverty in America. I guess I was blind to the facts because I always had clean clothes, food to eat, and family around no matter where I lived. I didn't know that the federal government was providing my family with special incentives at the expense of the taxpayers.

Once I realized that we were living in poverty, I felt like it was my duty to rescue myself and my family from it. Another thing I noticed during my time in the Deep South was that a lot of people seemed content with their circumstances. People rarely talked about leaving the town to start a new life or starting a business to create some wealth. Of course there's always exceptions, I knew several people that lived above the poverty line and they were all well-educated and well-traveled. These were the people that I strived to be like. I would pay close attention to everything from how they walked, talked, and dressed, to how they sat at the dinner table and prayed before meals. It's sad to say but people that lived like this were often accused of not being black enough. I'm not sure what that means but it's almost like the black people that made it out of poverty were always accused of thinking they are better than everyone else. I'm still trying to figure that one out which is another reason why I'm writing this book, to spark the conversation.

According to a report from the US Census Bureau, Income and Poverty in the United States: 2013, the median household income in for black households in 2013 was $34,598, $40,963 for Hispanic, $58,270 non-Hispanic white, and $67,065 Asian. I find it interesting that you see more black people in the sports and entertainment industry than any other race, yet blacks still struggle against poverty in the United States. What do you think this is saying about black people in the United States? Are we not applying ourselves enough? Are we looking for someone to blame for our problems or are we looking for the solutions? Yes, racism still exists, always will, and so will hatred and ignorance in the world. I'm not discounting the fact that slavery existed in the United States followed by segregation, then racism around de-segregation right afterwards. Today, there are countless opportunities for people of all races to become successful and achieve wealth. I said all that to say that this is not a book about race but more importantly a book about good decisions and thought patterns that I have used in reaction to growing up in a negative environment. My reaction to poverty has not always been a positive one but now I know better and you will too after reading this book. I want you to know that you are in control of how you choose to react to bad things that occur in your life. The real enemy, poverty doesn't care about race, religion, or anything else. Just like chess, poverty just wants to take out the king (you).

It's almost like I was programmed to believe that I should be fighting myself and others because of my family's financial situation. Later in life I learned that spreading love and gaining knowledge is the real key to defeating poverty. Now, I'm a firm believer in the phrase, "When you know better, you do better"! Are black people in America not doing better because we've been taught what to think instead of how to think? Are we teaching our children the same thing as other races? What's causing the inequality in the median household income? The smart thing to do is start finding ways to answer questions like these because poverty is here to stay. The ultimate question is what are we going to do about it? Poverty in America has gotten out of control, and it's time to do something about it. It's obviously not just a black thing and we don't have to re-invent the wheel to fix it. In fact, I believe it's never been about race; however race has been and will always be a hot topic that will generate interest amongst the public. In America we get all worked up over race, but in my opinion it's all smoke and mirrors now because the hard part has been done. People like Harriet Tubman, Martin Luther King Jr., Malcom X, and the many other civil rights activists have made sacrifices for the rights and freedoms that black people in America benefit from today. The same way those great people fought for civil rights, we have to fight poverty in America. It all starts with personal development and serving the community. We all have to do our part and if enough people join the fight, America will be a better place to live for everyone.

EARLY LIFE

It was the summer of 1983 and for some odd reason I can remember it like it was yesterday. My cousin Richard and I were sitting on a white baby blanket in the back of my grandmother's yard on the Southside of Chicago. As we sat there smiling waiting for the person behind a polaroid camera to snap our picture, I remember smelling the fresh cut grass and hearing the sound of birds chirping and various insect noises while Richard and I constantly squirmed and squinted our eyes because the sun was shining the brightest. I have encountered several doubters over the course of my life that will debate the validity of this recollection, however it's my story and I'm sticking to it. It just happens to be my oldest memory which is why it can never be erased. This memory is pivotal in my life and I feel like my life has been submerged in African American culture because so much happened in Chicago, Mississippi, and Georgia as it pertains to the African American experience post slavery, post great migration, and post MLK assassination. This section of "Escape from Poverty" will outline some background information about my early life and you as the reader will begin to understand why I am mentally wired the way I have been all my life.

Chicago is my birth place and where I began my quest to understand life and what it means to be a black man born into a poor family in the United States. My mother Maxine Hill and my father Rodrick Love met in Chicago at the home of one of my aunts in 1980. Aunt Felicia's house or "Lil mama's house was often the place to be and there was always music blaring from an 8 track stereo, card games, dominoes, and a lot of smoking and drinking. This wasn't just the party spot for my parents; there were many different people whose families had migrated from the south that ended up in Chicago. It didn't matter what day of the week they would all frequent my aunt's home but especially on the weekends. I loved going to aunt Lil mama's because I had a bunch of cousins and people would bring their kids and we would all play in one room, often times the basement. My mother and father dated for a couple years, and then I was born in July of 1982, shortly after my father returned home from the Navy. Two years earlier my mother had migrated to Chicago from a small town in Mississippi called Minter City.

According to my mom, things were good between her and my father until shortly after I was born. She and my father began to argue and fight on a regular basis about trivial things. My mom was never a drinker although admitted to smoking pot with her cousins during those years. My father had always been a heavy drinker, but what he didn't realize was it was leading to the start of his drug habit. He thought nothing of it because it was the early 80's and everyone was experimenting and having a good time. From what my parents explained to me, that was what the 80's was all about, "having a good time" because black people were free and the wars were over. This was around the time that crack hit inner-cities and everyone was doing it because it was the cool and hip thing to do. There was no such thing as crack heads and addicts like we see today, everything was done on a social level back then. This is part of the reason why I'm a firm believer in the phrase,

"Too much of anything is bad for you".

A large part of our time in Chicago was spent living with other family members because my family never really had a place of our own. Now, there was this one place not far from my grandmother's house on Woodlawn that we lived at for a while, it was on 65th and Greenwood. It was a small studio apartment that I can remember very well. I can remember cruising around the kitchen in a walker when I was a baby and I also can remember my parents arguing and me not wanting to hear the yelling. On one particular occasion, my mother and I had returned from brief trip to Mississippi and my father began questioning me about everything that happened. I remember telling my father about a man named Willie that I saw my mother talking to. I was very upset about my mother talking to this man and in my mind I vowed to tell my father once I returned home to Chicago. What I didn't realize was that I was giving my father the fuel for his accusatory attacks that would be aimed at my mother throughout my childhood. In the 8 years that I lived in Chicago, this was the only time my family had our own place.

The first relative to open their doors to my family was my mother's aunt Cora Lee who lived with her six children. My cousins were various ages, some even my mother's age. Aunt Cora's house was the cornerstone for our whole family. There have been several family members who have stayed with her at one time or another. My aunt Cora Lee lived in Henry Horner Homes in Chicago. According to the United States statistics, Henry Horner was one of the worst public housing projects. The name of this housing project might ring a bell to you, remember the movie

Losing Isaiah? The Henry Horner Projects was the backdrop for the movie which helped launch the careers of Cuba Gooding Jr. and Halle Berry. I'm not sure who my father was living with at the time but, by the time my little sister Shalundra was born and we were living in my aunt's house. This was where I learned the famous phrase "hit the floor" which was used often as a safety response to the frequent gunshots outside the home.

Henry Horner Homes sat on the Westside of Chicago and was a hot bed for criminal activity that included gang violence, prostitution, and major drug activity. I attended a school called Dett elementary which was a stone's throw away from the projects. I can remember walking home from school with my cousins and sometimes running for whatever reason. The time spent here was not as bad as it may seem because there was an overwhelming amount of love in the household. I always had someone to talk to at my aunt's house and someone was always talking or cracking jokes, most of the time it was my aunt Cora. She was tough and didn't take any mess from anyone. It seems kind of ironic but this is one of the places that I felt the safest, despite the fact that we were in one of the worst ghettos in America.

The second family we lived with was my mother's brother Willie, his wife Daphne, and their three children. My older cousins, Raymond and Shawn, didn't really mind me being there as long as I didn't mess with their stuff or go in there rooms. I knew that if I did that there would be hell to pay because these guys were tough, or at least I thought they were. I really liked living there because my cousin Chris was the youngest of the three and we are a year apart. It was like having a little brother and I had someone who I could talk to and understood me. We were best friends growing up and we did just about everything together from foot races, riding skateboards, to playing hide and seek with the kids in the neighborhood. My personal favorite was going to other kids' birthday parties and doing the Kid N Play dance moves. Chris and I were a one-two punch like Siskel and Ebert.

During this time I was attending Dumas elementary school on the south side of Chicago. I can remember wanting to go to Wadsworth which was the same school my cousin Chris attended because for some reason I thought it was more fun and the girls were prettier. I can remember being jealous of my cousin Chris because he had everything I wanted as a kid. My uncle Willie and aunt Daphne both had good jobs. They were the epitome of a nuclear family because they had a nice home, a dog, and my cousin Chris always had the best toys. Despite my true feelings, I never let this envy show because I loved them so much and I was so happy when I was around my cousin and his family. Deep down inside my mother always knew how I felt and I believe she felt guilty because she couldn't give me all the things I wanted as a child.

The one person that I can remember from this time that did give me everything I wanted was my grandfather Alfred. This was my dad's father and I worshiped the ground he walked on because he was always nice to me and he would always give me snacks when my family and I visited him in the nursing home. He was always smiling and he called me "Eh Eh" so much that I began to believe that this was my name. My grandfather Alfred was the only person that ever called me by that nickname, in fact I forgot about it until I started writing this passage. When my grandfather Alfred died, I realized that no one lives forever and started to become curious of what life was all about and why people have to die. This was the first funeral that I had ever been too in my life and I didn't really understand the meaning of life and death. I remember being upset at my sister, Shalundra, who was playing and picking her nose at our grandfather's funeral. I remember thinking to myself, "Doesn't she know that she is supposed to be sad right now". My parents were both crying and sad, therefore I felt like it was my responsibility to pay attention to my little sister. After the funeral everyone gathered at my Aunt Felicia's house and I was very confused at the end of this day because the whole family went to her house and had a party, at least it felt like one to me. This is where I learned how African Americans mourned lost love ones with a celebration in the person's honor.

By 1990, we had moved with the last set of relatives and stayed there before leaving Chicago for good. This time we lived with my (Dad's brother) uncle Dwight, aunt Barbara, and my three cousins (Kesha, Derrinda, and Ashley). My uncle and his family were kind enough to let us live in their attic for a while. My mom was pregnant with my baby brother Darius at the time, Shalundra, my sister, was about four years old, and I was eight years old at the time. I can recall living in their attic for a short period of time. The room was fairly big and was made of wood panel walls and it always kept a cool draft. With the room being upstairs, we had to go downstairs whenever we had to use the bathroom. My cousin Derrinda and I were closer in age so we walked to school together every day. I attended Fort Dearborn elementary school with my cousins and they were very popular. The school was on the Southside of Chicago but it felt like a different city because it seemed far away from where we had lived on 65th St.

I was attending Fort Dearborn when I witnessed my first school fight. My cousin Derrinda had literally stomped a girl out on the playground. I can remember my cousin being cheered on during the fight and congratulated after winning the fight by a landslide. This is when I realized that I had to be tough while going to school. My mindset was, if my girl cousins knew how to fight then I should know how to fight and be even tougher. Even though everyone knew that I had these tough girl cousins at

Fort Dearborn, I was kind of shy. Frankly, I was just tired of going to different schools and wanted my family to have a place of our own. I was tired of being homeless and this is where I realized that every family needs a place to call home.

    At the start of the second semester of my third grade year, I moved to Mississippi while my family stayed in Chicago. I never knew why I was the only one to separate from the family but I did. I moved in with my auntie Emma Jean, her husband David, and my cousins Dwayne, Shenedra, and Ophelia. Growing up I always thought my aunt Emma was the meanest person in the world because she wore a mean look all the time and often yelled when she talked. Also, Aunt Emma always had a few thin broken tree branches lying around the house just in case she needed to discipline anyone. One thing I realized fast about Mississippi was that there was a completely different dialect than what I was accustomed to growing up in Chicago. Everyone either talked extremely fast or extremely slow. Another interesting observation about the southern dialect was that Ebonics was prevalent. It was like learning a whole new language. I would often ask my cousins for translations of what people were saying to me. Every time I opened my mouth people would ask me, "where you from?"

Still in my third grade year of elementary school, I was enrolled at W.C.Williams elementary school next to the housing projects where we resided. The projects in Mississippi was nothing like the projects in Chicago, there were no high rises, no prostitutes on the corners, no broken glass on the ground, and everyone had their own yards. As for my new school, I knew fitting in wouldn't be an issue because I had become a professional at being the new kid in class. Before the first day at W.C. Williams my mind was made up, there would be no kid cooler, funnier, smarter, or tougher than me. I even gave myself a new nickname ..."D." For some reason, I felt like having this new nickname would somehow make me cooler and tougher. I made a lot of friends at this new school with my new found coolness and especially with the introductions my cousins gave every time I met one of their friends! I didn't stay at W.C.Williams for long because by the end of the school year my family had moved from Chicago to Decatur Georgia and they were waiting for me to rejoin them and I was ready to do just that!

Georgia was the place where I realized the significance of relationships. It was 1991, and I was starting the fourth grade at Kelly Lake elementary. I was so happy to be with my family again and I had cousins around my age so I didn't feel like a social misfit anymore. After living in Chicago and Mississippi for a short period of time, I was a professional at making people like me. I had figured out that I was in control of how I wanted others to perceive me. I immediately scoped the scene out to see who the coolest kids in school were and who the prettiest girls were. I knew that I had to get a beautiful girlfriend because they were usually the smart ones that were well known in school at least that's how it was in the schools I attended. The girl I dated and I can't really call it dating because I knew nothing about dating, plus we were little kids at home with our parents. Anyways, my new found girlfriend was my cousin's best friend and we would talk on the phone sometimes as if there was really something for us to talk about at 8 and 9 years old. I developed strong feelings for this young lady and I knew that this was something that I wanted for the rest of my life; to be in a relationship with someone I care about. It really broke my heart when we had to move away but I will continue with my time in Georgia. At school, I befriended two of the coolest guys in the school (Gary & Cortez) and I was immediately accepted amongst my peers. By this time I felt like I was a big boy because I used to ride my bike to my grandmother's house and sometimes to other parts of East Decatur. I can even remember walking my little sister to school and teaching her how to spell her name along the way. I always felt like I was responsible for taking care of my little sister and she worshiped the ground I walked on growing up.

While living in Georgia, I remember feeling like I was a super hero and I used to wonder if I was a descendant of a King because I felt like I was special. Despite all the arguing and fighting that I constantly heard my parents doing every day, I knew that God had a plan for me. When I would go outside and play baseball and footrace with my friends, I was always one of the fastest and one of the most coordinated of my friends. Everyone in Georgia was really into baseball and I picked up the sport with ease. We would find any open field or lot and literally play baseball with a tennis ball and a stick. We would make the bases out of anything you could find on the ground and as long as the person touched the base while running on offense or tagged the base while on defense, we were playing real baseball in our minds. I can also remember collecting baseball, basketball, and football cards. Now that was the thing to do in Georgia, you were nobody if you didn't collect trading cards, and that's what we did all the time, traded cards. I had only been living in Georgia for about a year before I started hanging out with the wrong crowd. I remember getting caught stealing cap guns in South DeKalb mall with some people that I thought were friends. Now that's a butt whipping that I will never forget because I got whipped by my mother in the mall security office, then once I got home my father whipped me to sleep. That same night, I cried myself to sleep and I vowed to never take anything that wasn't mine ever again. I learned many valuable lessons during my time in Georgia, but one of my fondest memories was when I learned the word entrepreneur. I remember being at a family gathering at my grandmother Hattie's house and I told her that

I was going to be an entrepreneur. I must have seen a commercial on television or saw the word somewhere but when I said it everyone laughed at me, probably because they knew I couldn't spell the word entrepreneur, in fact I still struggle with spelling it, but I was so serious that day. Even at my young age, I knew that if people were going to address me as an entrepreneur, it meant I was somewhat successful. It's funny because my 83 year old grandmother still reminds me of that same conversation to this day and it's always served as the only confirmation I needed from family. My grandmother believed me and that's all that mattered. I recently mentioned the conversation to a friend and to prove my claim to be true, I called my grandmother on the phone mid-story and she politely corroborated my story while on speakerphone. At this stage of life, I became curious about the kind of jobs the adults around me had.

Around the time my brother Darius was born in August of 1992, I had a strong feeling that my family and I were going to be leaving Georgia soon, which we did. I started to see all the same signs I saw before leaving Chicago. The main signs were the constant fights and arguments and my mother always had a sad look in her eyes. One day I overheard my mother on the phone talking about her dad in Mississippi being sick and shortly after my mother, sister, brother, and I were all on a greyhound bus headed down south leaving my dad behind in Georgia. I can remember the images inside the bus station as if it were yesterday. Many of the people had this restless look on their faces, some were traveling with big black plastic bags filled with clothes, and I remember seeing several other mother's traveling with small children like my mother. The bus trip seemed like an eternity because the bus had to stop in every small town it passed between Georgia and Mississippi. When I finally arrived in Mississippi during the summer of 93, ironically there was a feeling of relief. I knew that it would take a while to adjust to my new surroundings because the town looked as if it had been frozen in time. I remember entering the city and seeing a sign that read "Welcome to Greenwood, Mississippi, Cotton Capitol of the world". This just made me think about the old stories that I would hear about people picking cotton and it also made me think about those movies that we would watch in school during black history month. It was at that very moment that I realized that my family was poor and didn't have many options. I knew that I had to make friends fast and make the most of this tough situation. I had three goals when I got to Mississippi, learn everything about the people, learn everything about the place, and plan my escape.

I started school at Davis Elementary school on the Northwest side of Greenwood. I noticed that everyone at school looked like me; by this I mean everyone was black except for some of the teachers. I was quickly taken in by my peers because I had a handful of cousins at the school and everyone knew them. My cousins helped me lay a foundation with the "in-crowd" that carried me all the way to junior high and high school. We had lived with my Aunt Shirley, her son Jonathan, and my grandfather, in a big brown house on Strong Avenue during the first few years in Greenwood. Over the course of living there my mother and father had been communicating and it was around 95 when my dad moved to Mississippi. We rented a small house across the street from my aunt because my mother was still helping take care of my grandfather. I remember having mixed feelings about my father moving down because I remember all the fights my parents used to have in Chicago and Georgia. I thought things would be different and I'm sure my mother did too, because my dad would always sound nice and sincere on the telephone, he always did have the gift of gab.

By 1996, I was a freshman in high school, my sister was in 5th grade, and my brother was in the first grade. I was beginning to realize that my parents mostly argued over money and that we had some serious problems going on at home. My father would stay out late and come in and out of the house whenever payday rolled around. I used to try and catch him early on payday if I was going to get some cash from him because I knew that if I caught him the next day, he would claim that he was broke. I started to put everything together when I found a partially burned aluminum can under the bathroom sink. The can had a perfectly round hole punched on the side of it and I knew that it had to be drug related. I knew my father was doing something more than beer and cigarettes because he always had a different demeanor when he had money in his pockets and his mouth would stiffen up when he talked. Another thing that gave it away was the fact that he would argue with my mother over money that he had just given her for bills. This was also the time I joined a gang and began experimenting with drugs on a regular basis. My friends and I would get together and smoke marijuana every chance we got. The gang I joined was called The Four Horsemen and they had been around since 92 with about 200 members. During the first day of my initiation, there were almost 30 people trying to join with me and after two weeks of getting physically and mentally tortured, only five guys were initiated. Legend has it; I was one of the smallest yet toughest guys to ever get initiated into the four horsemen. The main reason I joined was because I wanted to solidify my place in the "In-crowd" and I knew that I could use the protection of some of the older, wiser, tougher members.

Throughout my time in high school I tried to play both sides of the fence. I wanted to hang with the smart kids and still be able to deal with the thugs in the street. I had played around the first couple years in school and let my grades slip. I was high on marijuana every day and I wanted to be the class clown and talk to the girls during class time. By my junior year, I was actually able to recover though. I found my balance between home and school life through building relationships. I was always in a healthy relationship and I had lots of friends. I even had friends that were in rival gangs and this meant that I was safe because I was well connected. My fascination with beautiful and smart women was one of my saving graces, largely because if I was at my girlfriend's house, I was safe and out of trouble. My philosophy was simple; if you have a girlfriend that's beautiful and smart that no one can take away, it will earn you respect! Well, that was exactly what happened, I dated some of the prettiest and smartest girls to ever pass through the junior high and high schools I attended and I was respected for that. Not to mention the fact that I was gang-affiliated, smart, dressed nice, and I was a ladies man. I also started working at the local grocery store once I turned 16, so I had my own money to do whatever I wanted. Luckily I was able to finish high school with a full scholarship to anywhere in the United States, in addition to a $3,000 book scholarship from the Greenwood Junior Auxiliary. From the outside looking in, I seemed like a normal kid growing up in the Mississippi Delta but I was going through so much turmoil at home. The constant fighting and arguing had started to take a toll on my sister, brother, and myself. I think we all dealt with our anger differently but for the most part we all kept it bottled up. I started to stand up to my father when the arguing ensued and this eventually led to a big fight that ended with a restraining order against my father. When my father moved away, I felt like a weight was lifted off my shoulder because I was tired of wondering if something bad would happen to my mother. Now that my father was gone, I felt like my family was no longer in danger and it was safe for me to leave Mississippi and begin my journey for success.

In 2002, I left for Charlotte, North Carolina to live with my uncle Phil for the summer. It was the beginning of a whole new life for me and I remember feeling hopeful about my future. Everything about Charlotte just felt right so I asked my uncle if I could stay with him for good. That same summer I took a trip down to Mississippi, packed everything I owned into my 1993 Chevrolet Corsica and made the journey back to Charlotte. I began attending the University of North Carolina at Charlotte that fall and I got a job at a shoe store in the mall near my uncle's house. I only worked at the shoe store for enough time to make a few friends that I built my core social network around. I also became the number one salesperson at the shoe store which caused me set my sights on a serious career in sales. I had a cousin around my age that I often hung out with so I felt right at home in Charlotte. Everything about Charlotte felt right and for the first time in my life there was no fear of poverty, anger, or sadness. After living with my uncle for less than a year I decided to get a place of my own. By this time I landed a job at the Bose Corporation which opened so many doors professionally and I was making more money than both my parents had ever made in their whole lives working. I was able to travel and accomplish a lot over the six years working for the Bose Corporation. I received some of the best professional mentoring and training and I left with a resume full of accomplishments. Some of the accomplishments include: meeting Dr. Bose himself, becoming the employee of the year for the retail direct group in 2006, number one retail store in America in 2006, and Runner-up to number one store in 2007. During these years, I learned how to be self-sufficient and I was also able to help my family back home in Mississippi.

In 2007, I was 25 years old and having the time of my life. This was the same year I met my wife, Shapera at a gas station near the University of North Carolina at Charlotte. I remember it like it was yesterday because I had just taken my younger brother Darius to his first Rock and Roll concert. Darius was a senior in high school in Mississippi and I wanted to make sure he had some great stories to tell his friends about his summer in Charlotte. I was also planting a seed in my brother so that he will see what life is like outside of Mississippi and what happens when you work hard. It was also in the year 2007 that my father was diagnosed with prostate cancer which was a very humbling experience. I had always felt like there was a hole in my heart that had to be filled if I was going to ever achieve success. I had to rid myself of all any ill feelings towards my father and forgive him for what I was holding on to from the past. It was time to stop feeling sorry for myself about the life I didn't have growing up and start working on the future of my dreams. I also knew that there was still a lot I wanted to learn from my father and questions that I wanted to ask about his past. When I started repairing my relationship with my father it was then I began to release all hate in my heart. The decision to let my father back into my heart was difficult, but I knew it was necessary. I really wanted to show my father that he had support during this difficult time in his life. I learned so much from my father over the next 7 years after that and his words often echo in my head, especially when I'm making a difficult decision.

When I buried my father in January 2014, I realized that he was with me my whole life teaching me lessons. Even in the situations where I was learning what not to do, I was lucky enough to have him as part of my life. It has been proven that so many young black males have been abandoned by someone at one time or another. No matter your race, if you've ever felt abandoned by anyone, whether it was your parents, your friends, society, or if you just feel like you've been written off, this book is for you. Don't pay attention to what the statistics have to say about people that come from poverty. Let my testimony serve as an inspiration to be what you want to be in life. Who cares what the statistics say? Forget what the media says about the people in your neighborhood? I don't care about statistics and neither should you! All the sacrifices and challenges that I've faced in life make sense now because they made me who I am today. Everything happens for a reason and what doesn't kill you only makes you stronger. In order to truly escape from poverty, you have to look deep within yourself, become a life-long learner, think positively, and remove the mental chains that have been placed upon you by society. I've seen many loved ones fall victim to poor health, death, incarceration, drug abuse, and lack of will power for fear of poverty. Don't allow yourself to fall victim to these things and pay close attention to the chapters that you are about to read in this book.

GOD FIRST

"If you keep God first, you can't help but win at everything you do"

Isn't it interesting when you hear someone say I'm not religious but I'm spiritual. This has become the popular thing to say these days. Is it really just another way of saying that I'm focused on myself at the moment and I don't have time for God? Or, are people truly connecting with a higher power through meditation and prayer within themselves? I can't blame the spiritual people for feeling this way though. Religion has become a profession these days and it's being bought and sold to the highest bidder on every street corner. Please don't get me wrong I'm not attacking anyone that's religious or spiritual because I am in no position to judge. I am simply saying that we need to remember to put God first no matter what our beliefs are. This is especially important if you're going to put the idea of poverty in your rear view mirror for good.

I do find it interesting that some religious people are so focused on what they are going to wear to church and what songs the choir will sing. All this and once they walk out of church they can't tell you one verse the pastor used in the sermon, yet they'll be the first one to greet you with a hallelujah the next day. The spiritual person on the other hand won't think twice about going to church because they are too busy saying, "my body is the temple...so I'm just going to sit here on the couch and watch ESPN or the lifetime movie channel." or "All the sinners are in the church, so I'm not going!" It all really boils down to one thing, we as humans want to do what we want to do...and most of us really don't really care what anyone else thinks about us...including God! Have you ever stopped and asked yourself, "I wonder if God is pleased with the way that I have been living my life?" We've all heard the saying... "The truth hurts". You have to be honest with yourself and admit that you have been living for yourself and not for God!

For some, the moment you fall in love and for others the moment you have children, you begin to love another person more than you love God and yourself. I can recall when my daughter was born and I brought her home on my 30th birthday...The first thing I did when we got home was call my mother and apologize for everything. Yes, I apologized for everything because I know there had to be something that I had done in the past that she was not very pleased with. The funny thing is that I had no idea what that thing was... I was just so happy that I was being trusted by God to take care of another human being! It was at this moment that I realized how much my parents loved me and also how much God loved me! It was all a part of God's plan for me to learn this valuable lesson about loving God. So...I have come to the conclusion that whether you are spiritual or religious, no-one and no-thing should come before God! Not your spouse, not your children, and not even your parents should be placed before God! If you keep God first for all of your days, you are sure to be successful at escaping from poverty.

Chess Move # 1: Make time throughout the day to pray and talk to God. This will help you develop a direct line to the creator. Don't wait for things to go wrong before you talk to God. You can pray while you are driving, when you're walking down the street, while you're taking out the trash, it doesn't matter as long as you make time.

I LOVE ME SOME ME

"Love yourself as you want to be loved"

Loving yourself is the most important thing you can do to escape from poverty and win at life. Self-love impacts happiness more than any other emotion. Most people that lack self-love are unhappy with several areas of their life and it shows. If you don't love yourself, how can you expect anyone else to love you? Self-love affects everything you do in life and it also affects everyone around you. Don't hurt the people that love you by not taking care of yourself. Love has to begin inside you in order for it to be expressed outwardly. You will notice that good things will begin to happen in your life when you have self-love. When I was growing up in the struggle, I would constantly say to myself, "I love you Eddie; your situation will be better one day". No matter my financial situation, I have always kept an optimistic outlook on life and a positive impression of myself. If you are going to attract wealth, love, or happiness, it's essential for you to love yourself.

Here are three ways to practice self-love on a daily basis:

1. Give yourself compliments

Every time you pass a mirror give yourself a compliment and say, "I love me some me!" No one should make you feel better about your life than you. When you wake up in the morning, the first thing you should do is say "I'm amazing, talented, and I feel good today!" If you start each day with compliments and positive affirmations, you don't have to wait for others to compliment you. You will already have that reassurance that you are one of God's beautiful creations.

2. Take care of your body

A large part of loving yourself involves taking care of your body. Make sure that you are getting the medical attention that you need on a regular basis so that you can live a long healthy life. Avoid using drugs and putting toxins into your body because these things will kill you. Watch the food that you eat in order to stay healthy. If you are getting all the nutrients and vitamins you need, you're able to function better. Healthy eating promotes brain function and increases energy levels. Working out is also something that you can do to make yourself feel better about life. There are a lot of outdoor activities that you will find both fun and healthy such as running, swimming, hiking, or playing basketball. Taking care of your body will make you feel good about yourself and show others that you love yourself.

3. Learn to forgive yourself

Don't allow yourself to be held hostage by your past experiences. If you feel guilty about something from your past, it's time to let it go. Don't allow your conscience to block you from achieving self-love. Everything that happens in life is for a reason and sometimes you have to pause and analyze why certain things have occurred. Ask yourself what was the lesson I had to learn? How do I move forward? If you want to experience self-love, you must let go and let God!

Many people feel like it's the responsibility of someone else to make them happy but that's untrue. While growing up in poverty, I never struggled with self-love. During this time I learned that the people closest to you have the power to hurt you the most. Keep in mind that you give people power over you when you rely on them to make you happy. Don't make it easy for people to take advantage of you. People will tell you everything you want to hear especially if they sense that you have a lack of self-love. This is why you must take full responsibility for loving yourself in order to live a happy and prosperous life.

Chess Move #2: Spend some time with yourself today. Treat yourself to a nice meal or just go out and have some fun. Show people how you want them to treat you by spending quality time with yourself.

REPROGRAM YOUR MIND

"The first thing you need to do in order to reprogram is deprogram"

If you stuck your hand inside a jar of jelly, could you touch the sweetness? If I stuck my hand inside your head, could I touch your mind? Of course, the answer to both questions is no. I would have to taste the jelly to know whether it's sweet. Touching your mind would be impossible because I could only touch your brain. The mind is internal and only you have access to it. The mind is like a hidden treasure because it has so many precious jewels waiting to be discovered. All you have to do is create a map and start the journey of reprogramming your mind. The map is represented by the goals that you are focused on achieving. The journey is represented by the hard work involved with discovering your minds hidden abilities. I knew that I was going to use my mind if I was going to change my future. I wasn't going to let society and statistics define how my story will end. When I took possession of my mind I began to pull away from the pack. I say pull away from the pack because people are much like crabs in a bucket. Everyone is stuck at the bottom of the barrel and all doing the same thing which is trying to pull each other down. The harder the crab tries to escape from the bottom of the bucket, the harder the other crabs will fight to pull him back down. What are you going to do different to make sure you don't end up like all the other crabs? The answer to this question is the key reason I was able to escape from poverty. The answer is seems simple but is very hard to do and even harder to sustain. Your ultimate weapon to defeat poverty is reprogramming your mind.

The first thing you need to do to reprogram is to deprogram. What do I mean by this? We live in a very controlled society and everyone does what they think they should be doing or what they've been told to do. If someone were to ask you why do you go to work every day, how would you answer? Do you go to work because everyone else does? Or, do you go because you need money? Either way, you are doing what everyone else does and just like them, you become a slave to society. You have become a slave because you stopped doing things for the passion and what growth and development will come from it. No, for you it's all about popular culture and money. When you allow yourself to become programmed you really don't know why you do the things you do. It's like living inside a bubble! The people that live in the bubble allow the media to dictate their political party. These same folks drive a certain car because everyone in Hollywood drives it. Programmed people rely on popular magazines to tell them what beauty and fashion should look like. It's like they are zombies trapped in a system of mind control. If you don't take the time to think for yourself, someone else will always do it for you.

How do you deprogram? The answer is simple; you have to turn off the noise. The noise is all the unimportant information that you are exposed to each day. The noise is anything that doesn't mean you any good. It can be anything from a bad relationship to the 10 o'clock news. I say the news because noise can come from anywhere and is often sandwiched in with good things. Every time I watch the news, I get upset because they never report on the positive things that happen in communities nationwide. It's always something about crime, politics, and money. You can be listening to your favorite song on the radio and the next song you hear is degrading to women by calling them every name but what they are. If something is causing you to feel negative emotions like anger, fear, or depression, it falls in the category of noise! Like I said, noise can come from anywhere so be ready to shut it off.

Now, let's talk about how to reprogram because this is what the chapter is about. After you have shut the noise down by deprogramming, the next step is to reprogram. In order to reprogram your mind, you need to establish new daily rituals which involve feeding yourself positive information. You must be conscious of what you're taking into your mind from the beginning of your day to the end. The first ritual should be to read something positive during the first hour that you're awake. In Psychology of Achievement, Brian Tracy calls the first hour you wake up the golden hour because it's when you brain is working the hardest and you set the tone for your day. You're trying to remember what you dreamed about last night, what clothes to put on for work, what for breakfast, lunch, dinner, and a lot of other things I'm sure! If you feed your mind good wholesome information first thing in the morning, you will always start on a good note. The second ritual to help you reprogram your mind is to create a vision board. The vision board will send your mind images of the things you want to achieve. You should surround yourself with these images. They should be on the refrigerator, in your car, and on your desk at work if you have one. Looking at these images will remind you of what you're striving for. This will help ease the pain of hard work because nothing worth having in life comes easy. The last thing you must do in order to reprogram is to become a life-long learner. Every opportunity you get to learn something new, take advantage of it. Personal development guru Zig Ziglar always talked about automobile university, which caused me to invest a great deal of money into audiobooks. Since I did this, every time I get into my car, I'm learning because I don't play music unless someone is riding with me. You should enroll in a course at a local college or get a certification in something you've always been interested at learning. There are workshops and seminars that you can attend for free and nowadays you can just go to the internet if you want to learn something.

The key to reprogramming is to keep it positive. There is enough negativity in the world to go around and you will absorb a lot of it indirectly. This means, whether you want to entertain negativity or not, it will be forced upon you by people and the world around you. The best thing you can do is control what you can control and that's your mind. If making a lot of money is your only idea of success, you are in for a rude awakening. You have to take control of your mind if you are going to sustain wealth. As the old saying goes, "A fool and his money are soon parted". Don't be like the crabs in the world and hang out at the bottom of the bucket! Take the time to reprogram your mind and you can kiss poverty goodbye and good riddance, that's what I did and now I'm winning!

Chess Move #3: Use the first fifteen minutes each morning to meditate. This will help you clear your mind and quite the noise in your head and all around you. It will allow you to have a moment of peace which how you want to remain throughout the day.

CREATE A VISION

"Your life will always be a blur to others if your vision is not clear"

Is your vision 20/20? No, I'm not talking about your eyesight, I'm talking about the vision that you have for your life. What are you doing right now to prepare for your future? In 2008 when the United States faced an economic downturn, my life was impacted in a major way. Before the downturn, I was living the bachelor life and I thought I had it all figured out. The problem was that I was living in the moment and I wasn't focused on the future. I wasn't concerned with the steps I would have to take if I ever ran into a rainy day. Yes, I had a couple thousand in my savings account and I had over

$15,000 in my 401k. In my mind this was all I needed and as long as I was able to jump into my nice car with rims on it, crank up my banging sound system, wear flashy overpriced clothing, and party with my friends all night, I was doing great for myself. For a young guy, I felt like I was ahead of the game and poverty was in my rear view mirror until a rude awakening happened, which was the housing bubble and stock market crash. During this time I had a series of humbling events happen to me and I had no plan to fix any of them. To name a few; my father was diagnosed with prostate cancer, I was in the early stages of what was becoming a serious relationship, I dropped out of college during the second semester of my senior year, I quit my job at one of the world's largest retailers where I was a manager, my car got totaled, I moved out of my bachelor pad and into one of the roughest neighborhoods in Charlotte, my 401k was getting gobbled up because it was diversified in the stock market, and I was on the verge of calling my mother to say I'm moving back home to Mississippi. I was so consumed in the worldly mess that I had created and my life lacked real substance because I didn't take time to create a vision. I didn't know what my next move was going to be but I knew I had to do something and do it quickly!

What did I do to get past this critical point in my life? I can recall a conversation that I had with my wife in 2009 who was my girlfriend at the time. Her exact words were, "You need to figure out what you want in life and stop looking for a pity party!" Those words hit me like a ton of bricks and at that very moment I realized what I really wanted to do in life and I started working on my vision. The first thing that I did was pull the goals out of my head by writing them down. I asked myself four specific questions which were: What are my goals? How will I achieve this? Who will inspire me? Why do I want this? By pulling my goals out of the mental chaos inside my head, I made my goals become both physical and mental. How many times have you come up with a great idea while driving but forget what it is by the time you reach your destination? By writing down my goals I was able to touch them, speak them, hear them, and almost taste them! It was like my vision came to life when I wrote down my goals!

How do you create your vision? I suggest talking to a life coach, counselor, or friend to start out. This allows you to vent to another human being and get everything that's been blocking your vision out of your system. Next you have to write down your goals and ask yourself the four questions: What are my goals? How will I achieve this? Who will inspire me? Why do I want this? It doesn't matter whether those goals are short term or long term just make sure they are specific, measurable, attainable, realistic, and time phased, which is called the SMART method. You can even create two goal lists, one for short term and another for long term. The next thing I suggest that you do is surround yourself with the list. By this, I mean place a copy of your goals on the night stand in your bedroom, in the car, on the refrigerator, at your job, or anyplace you spend a lot of time. You will find yourself thinking about your goals from the time you wake up until the time you go to bed at night. When you do this, you will begin to pull away from the pack of dreamers and create a habit of winning as you accomplish small victories and cross things off the list. Since we're on the topic of dreamers, watch out for the dream killers because they will reveal themselves one by one. Many people allow their vision to get blurred by the dream killers and let their passion burn out because they are too focused on what other people think of their vision. You can't give people any control over your vision and know that you will be judged by society all the time no matter what you do. If I always wanted to be a garbage man and I become a garbage man...no one can tell me that I'm not successful because this is my vision not theirs. I would be the best damn garbage man on the planet and I would be happy because I created a winning vision for my life.

Chess Move #4: Take a moment to write down your goals. When you write them down they become physical. There is simply too much traffic inside your head and you have to pull out the goals. If you keep all your plans inside your head, they will either be lost forever or you will never attempt them.

ACTIVATE FAITH

"In order to elevate, you must activate faith."

What does the word faith mean to you? According to Wikipedia, Faith is defined as belief, confidence or trust in a person, object, religion, idea, or view despite the absence of proof. Have you ever stopped and asked yourself this important question? The answer to this question, like most, largely depends upon who you ask. If you ask a person that's living in poverty, they will more than likely give you a religious or spiritual explanation. When I lived in poverty, I was constantly reminded that God is in control and that he will make a way for a better life. Also that faith was the only thing that would deliver my family from poverty. It was almost as if all we had to do was pray and everything would be alright, which is true in a sense; however I feel there's more to it than just praying. If you ask the same question to a person that's well off and has achieved a great deal of success they will probably define faith as the confidence or belief in one's self that's required to achieve whatever goal you set out to reach. Not to say that a person that's well off won't make the religious or spiritual connection, I'm simply saying that most successful people know that it takes prayer and belief but it also takes action in conjunction with the two.

Napoleon Hill, author of the best personal development book of all time, Think and Grow Rich, gave an excellent explanation on Applied Faith in his critically acclaimed video recording, The Master Key to Success. Hill called faith a mental attitude that we must cultivate and maintain if we are going to take full possession of our minds. Think and Grow Rich and The Master Key to Success were two of the major influences that led to me breaking the mental chains of poverty. My opinion is that faith has to be activated in order for it to work and the first way to activate faith is to look in the mirror and ask the question, what does faith mean to me? After you define what it means in your own words, the next step is to specify what you wish to achieve. Once you have asked yourself the question, specify what you are applying faith to. You can now begin to pray about whatever you wish to achieve. The last and final step to activating your faith is to create new habits around the idea that you are applying faith to. It's almost like you are building a sculpture and you tell yourself that

I'm going to chisel away at the design every morning at 6 am. By creating this new habit of waking up every morning to work on the sculpture you've activated the faith by not just thinking about it but doing something that will get you closer to the finished masterpiece. The new habits are going help you gain the confidence and belief in yourself as you move closer and closer to the life you want and whatever goal you wish to achieve because if you don't have faith in yourself, how can you expect anyone else to? Simply having faith is not enough to escape from poverty, you have to activate faith.

Chess Move #5: Speak favor over your life today! In order to activate faith in your life, you must learn to speak things into existence. You will notice that the universe will respond, once your voice sends the vibrations into the atmosphere. Here's something to think about, God told Moses what to say before the Red Sea was parted. Exodus 14:15: "Then the LORD said to Moses, "Why are you crying out to Me? Tell the sons of Israel to go forward."

TRUST YOUR INTUITION

"Always trust your intuition to guide you in the right direction"

What is intuition and why am I telling you to trust it? In my mind intuition is the universe speaking directly to you and through you. If you break down the human body we are made up of the same materials and particles that make up the universe. Everything from atoms, protons, and neutrons, to the structure of the galaxies mimics the make-up of the human body. Wikipedia defines intuition as: a phenomenon of the mind, describes the ability to acquire knowledge without inference or the use of reason. Wikipedia goes on to reference the following: In Hinduism various philosophers have tried to decipher the Vedic and other esoteric texts & have brought about various interpretation. Buddhism finds intuition being a faculty in the mind of immediate knowledge & puts the term intuition beyond mental process of conscious thinking, as the conscious intellect cannot necessarily access subconscious information, or render such information into a communicable form. In Islam there are various scholars with varied interpretation of intuition (often termed as hads, hitting correctly on a mark), sometimes relating the ability of having intuitive knowledge to prophet hood. In the West, intuition does not appear as a separate field of study, and early mention and definition can be traced back to Plato, in his book Republic he tries to define intuition as a fundamental capacity of human reason to comprehend the true nature of reality.

I can remember the first time I trusted my intuition as if it were yesterday. I was seventeen years old and it was the last week of school during my senior year. The seniors really didn't have to attend school this day because we were all graduating that Friday. The Thursday before the graduation we were scheduled to have a senior class awards banquet where different superlative awards would be given. I just knew that I was going to win a few awards this night because it was based on nominations from my peers. One of the daily rituals for me and a group of friends was to smoke marijuana before school. This particular day I woke up with an eerie feeling and I just felt like something was about to go wrong. I didn't quite know why I felt this way but I knew that I was going to listen to my intuition. When my ride pulled up at my house I got in the car and everyone was hype and ready. My friends were especially excited about smoking this day because it was the last week of school and we all knew that we didn't have to do much work when we got there. I can remember saying "I'm not smoking today" once I sat in the car and my buddies began to laugh and tease me. As my friends teased me for acting like a square, my mind was set on not smoking because of this feeling I felt. I couldn't explain what it was but it was so powerful and I could resist paying attention to it.

There were a few smoke spots that we would choose from each day but this particular day we chose the city park. As my buddies sat in the park smoking I chose to sit in the car and think. I knew that they were laughing at me and it looked like they were having a good time in the park. When they were halfway done smoking the blunt I decided to get out of the car and go sit with them on the park bench while they finished. I must have been on the bench for two minutes before a police car comes charging in our direction. The police was driving across the grass and was in a hurry to get to us almost like he was tipped off by an informant because he just knew we were up to something illegal. When the police got out of his car he immediately recognized a couple of my friends because they were standout players on the high school baseball team. I remember telling the police officer these exact words, "I know the bank robber story and I know that I'm guilty by association, however for the record, I didn't smoke". My friends never let me live that one down but in my head, all they had to do was listen to me and not smoke, we would never have gotten caught.

I had trusted my intuition that morning and predicted a negative situation but still managed to get in trouble. The police officer took down each our names and went to the school to report us to the principal. When my friends and I got to school, all of our names were called over the intercom and we all had to report to the office. We knew we were in trouble and we spotted each other in the hallways as we made our way to the principal's office to wait for our parents to pick us up. Part of our punishment was to miss the upcoming senior class night which we were all looking forward to that Thursday. I also had to deal with my buddies making fun of me for saying telling the police that I didn't smoke. I only did this to spare myself some of the trouble with my parents but I ended up in the same amount of trouble anyways and I remember thinking that I should have smoked!

If you're going to escape from poverty, you must be able to trust your intuition. Your inner self speaks to you all the time, especially when you're in a difficult situation. In difficult times, your mind is racing and it's hard to rationalize the next move but intuition will always be present. It's the inner voice inside your head that tells you the best possible solution to the problem. It's the gut feeling inside your body that adjusts with the mood or emotion that you're feeling at any given point in time. Intuition works hand and hand with your adrenaline and is controlled by your Amygdala. This is the part of your body located within the temporal lobes that determines if you fight or take flight in a difficult situation. Trusting your intuition is sort of like gambling but you should always bet on yourself if you're going to escape from poverty and win at life!

Chess Move #6: Make it a point to stop second guessing yourself and trust your intuition today. Here is passage from Thomas Troward's Edinburg h Lectures on Mental Science, *"The importance of understanding and following the intuition cannot be exaggerated, but I candidly admit the great practical difficulty of keeping the happy mean between the disregard of the interior voice and allowing ourselves to be run away with by groundless fancies. The best guide is the knowledge that comes of personal experience which gradually leads to the acquisition of a sort of inward sense of touch that enables us to distinguish the true from the false, and which appears to grow with the sincere desire for truth and with the recognition of the spirit as its source."*

THE POWER OF POSITIVITY

"Always have a positive disposition and you will never be a stranger"

There are arguably three types of people in the world, those who are extremely positive on a consistent basis, those who are extremely negative on a consistent basis, and those who are so far in the middle that they hardly express any emotion over anything. Napoleon Hill said it best, "Negative people see the hole in the donut, while positive people see the hole around the donut". When I lived in poverty in Chicago, I felt like I had to be optimistic in order to make it out. I always felt like I had a direct line of communication to God and that someday my life would be better and my family would have a place of our own. I never spent a great deal of time or energy on negativity when I was growing up in poverty; I spent most of my time focusing on building relationships and understanding communication. I learned how to see with my ears and listen with my eyes and this has always helped me to easily identify genuinely positive people. What I mean by this is I had to understand the importance of nonverbal communication and use visualization to put things into perspective. I knew that positive people moved about the world in a totally different way than the negative people and emotionless people. It was obvious to me that the positive people were usually successful because they had substance to their characters while on the other hand, the negative and emotionless people usually lacked substance. Positivity became a way of life for me at an early age and I knew that if I was going to better my circumstances I had to keep positive even on my bad days.

When you're always smiling and looking at the bright side of things, people will attract to you like a moth to a flame. This is because positive begets positive the same way that negative begets negative. Just think about it, you probably know someone that's always complaining and never happy, kind of like the donkey Eeyore from Winnie the Pooh. Every time this person comes around everyone hangs their head and murmurs "O Lord" under their breath. If you don't know a person like this it means that you are probably the negative person that no one wants to be around. Don't feel bad about it; you just need to change your attitude and your mindset. You must always look at the glass of water as half full and never half empty. Negative emotions tend to cloud your judgment and can cause you to miss important details. I'm sure you've been engaged in an argument or disagreement with someone close to you and the other person might have raised their voice at you because of frustration. Now I don't know about you but when someone yells at me, I tend to miss a lot of what they are saying because in my mind I am going into defense mode. Then I am trying to think of what I'm going to say next to combat the attack. When you really think about it, there is so much energy wasted on negativity because it only makes things worse no matter the situation.

When you express no emotion it usually tends to only make matters worse because someone is going to be left frustrated and confused. It's better to pick a side and you stand to gain much more by being on the positive side of things. When you have an I don't care attitude people are going to handle you any type of way because they know that it won't affect how you feel. You are basically giving people the right to treat you any kind of way. One of my favorite sayings has always been, "A man that stands for nothing will fall for anything". If you take the time to weigh the good against the bad in all situations you will live a much more balanced life if you always side with positivity. You will also live a much more successful life because studies have shown that happy people are usually more successful. If you need help with being positive hire a life coach, attend a seminar or workshop, or invest in books that will help you focus on positivity. Being positive is one of the most powerful ways to win against poverty and live a life of success and abundance.

Chess Move #7: Maintain a positive attitude throughout the day today. You will find yourself being much more productive in every activity or conversation you engage in. A little positivity can alter the future in an amazing way.

FACE YOUR FEARS

"The thought of climbing a mountain will deter you away from starting the climb; don't think about it, just climb."

The first thing that you must come to terms with in life is that everyone is afraid of something. Some people are afraid of dying, while others might be afraid of snakes or flying on airplanes. The best thing that you can do to overcome fear is simply live your life to the fullest. Go skydiving if you are afraid of airplanes. Maybe you need to visit a pet shop and just hold a snake for 5 seconds. The only way to overcome your fears is to face your fears head on! I know it's easier said than done but you must find a starting point if you're ever going to get past the fear. I've learned that when you face your fears in life, you will gain the necessary confidence required to accomplish the goals you've always dreamed of accomplishing. I was in denial for a long time because I would tell people, "I'm not afraid of anything" but the truth was that I was afraid of poverty. I never want to live in poverty again, which is one of the reasons I'm writing this book. My goal is to transfer my thoughts onto paper so that I can read them over and over again, while helping others at the same time. I want my legacy to be one of strength and courage. Facing your fears head on begins with determining what matters most to you in life. What are you good at? What makes you unique? What are your biggest opportunities for improvement? These are questions that only you can answer because no one knows you better than you! Don't allow yourself to keep everything bottled in and own up to what you are most afraid of. Sometimes you just need to vent and talk with someone, whether it's a life coach, a counselor, or a friend that's only going to listen and not judge you. In order to achieve the success that you've always dreamed of you must stare fear in the face and laugh!

Chess Move #8: Take the time to acknowledge your fears today! Write your fears down on a piece of paper because this will help you start the process of defining them. Once you have defined the fears, it will be easier to identify the desired outcome you wish to achieve.

JUST BE PATIENT

"Keep the boat steady as you sail to foreign lands"

Today we live in a world that glorifies material possessions and worldly things yet no one really wants to work hard to attain them. This idea is especially true in America, largely because we have pegged ourselves as the land of the free and a place where anything is possible. The whole idea of the American dream has been packaged and sold yet there are a lot of people that have been locked out of the dream. Our nation has been built on the principles of innovation and capitalism, but a lot of people have been on the opposite end of the success ladder. The people living in poverty either lack the resources, education, mindset, time, or all the above to achieve the American dream. There's only a small percentage that escape from poverty and achieve success in life and it's usually the ones that learn to master the art of being patient.

American culture has taught us that instant gratification is the way to go and fame can be yours if you get lucky! We want to drive the most expensive cars, live in the nicest homes, vacation at luxury resorts, and dine at five star restaurants. Even the people that don't have the means to live the glamourous life want to at least look the part because it's the thing to do. This just proves that no one has the will power to be patient and build their success foundation the right way. It almost seems like everyone has been programed to be in a rush and take shortcuts. The next time you go out into the world count the number of fast food restaurants and while you at it, notice the amount of people with smart phones. Even the little kids have smart phones these days, which means they can google anything at any time. Maybe this is why the Burger King slogan is so popular because everyone wants to have it their way. Are the days of working hard and saving pennies in a piggy bank gone? Is it all about hitting the jackpot now?

I believe you have to be patient as you execute your goals in life one by one. It's like building a house from the ground up, you must take your time and lay the foundation then carefully execute the rest of the plan. If the foundation is not laid properly, the house won't be as strong and it will cause you to adjust the blueprints. There are some people who marry well, while others inherit tons of money from rich family members. You might even be lucky and get discovered in the music industry like Justin Bieber. You can even blow up from social media because of its huge impact on popular culture! Between the blog sites and YouTube, all you have to do is be sure to have the proper lighting and editing and millions of bucks are just around the corner! The major point I want to make here is that patience is still a virtue. You have to take your time and plan things out properly. The problem today is that no one wants to be patient and wait for things to unfold properly because we want instant gratification. I'm sure you've heard the old saying, "good things come to those who wait", that's what has to happen if you're going to escape from poverty. You just have to be patient and do the work and as my mother would say to me, "Stay steady in the boat"!

Chess Move #9: Take your time today. Don't miss any deadlines but just slow down and be patient. If you are going to build anything of substance, you must take your time and lay the foundation first. As you continue to construct your masterpiece, make sure that each section is carefully inspected before moving to the next.

EDUCATE YOURSELF

"Over the course of your life, seize every opportunity to educate yourself"

We are all born with a blank slate, which philosopher John Locke refers to as tabula rasa. If you are blessed with all five senses, there is nothing stopping you from achieving success in life! Life is all about choices and outcomes. If you make the choice to educate yourself it will surely remove you from the ranks of poverty and change the expected outcome. In the old days you had to read stone tablets, and then scrolls made of leather or papyrus, next you had books, and now you have the World Wide Web. Not only do we use computers every day for work, most people have cellular phones, which nowadays are just miniature computers! This means that you constantly have a surplus of information at your fingertips.

One of the best lessons I've learned in life is that education should be a lifelong process. You should always be doing research and focusing on ways to improve your knowledge of general things. It's even better if you pick a specific area of focus and become an expert at it. When you educate yourself and become an expert at something you are increasing your personal stock value. You are also guaranteeing that you have a particular area that you can gain income from while building an empire in your spare time. This gives you something to fall back on just in case your plan doesn't work the way you intended.

A quote that my father used to often use was, "Learn a little bit about everything and you can talk to anybody". These words resonated with me and they have echoed through my head ever since I was a young boy. I can honestly say that this is the best lesson my father taught me and also what made me want to attend college. Going to college allowed me to expand my mind beyond everything I was taught in the years leading up to this point. For the first time in my life I felt like I was in control of what I had to study in order to be successful. I was amazed at the fact that I could pick what classes I wanted to take when I wanted to take them. College also taught me that I hadn't really learned anything about life! I soon realized that the world is full of information and there was just no reason for me to live in poverty again. I could learn about anything and make money from my knowledge. Whether your choice is to read books and self-educate, get a certification, attend college and get ten degrees, educating yourself will give you the power to win against poverty!

Chess Move #10: Spend one hour doing research today! Go to the internet and research a topic that you are passionate about. This is one of the best ways for you to become a subject matter expert on any topic.

SPREAD LOVE

"When you spread love into the universe, it will send love right back to you in a major way"

Spreading Love is sometimes hard to do because it may require you to face your fears and deal with a block that has been created from a difficult ordeal in your past. There may be a person or people that have hurt, wronged, or disappointed you and it's been hindering you from expressing how you really feel about people. When you let go of your ego and let God control your actions, it shows that you have learned how to deal with it (whatever happened) and them (whoever caused it). Moving forward means focusing on the solution and not the problem, you have to be optimistic about the future and use love and kindness in all your daily decisions. Holding grudges is not the way to happiness and the only person that ends up getting hurt is you. Sometimes people get trapped in poverty because they keep all the pain and sorrow from the past buried deep down within them. In most cases this negatively impacts the relationships in your life and can be devastating to your productivity and peace of mind.

I've always been a huge fan of Bob Marley because of his timeless and universal hit song One Love. The reason I love the song is because the words spoke clearly to me and had so much meaning. Marley's song helped me understand the importance of loving my neighbor. I've always seen the world for what it really is and that's a cultural melting pot. There are so many unique and interesting people in the world. It's our duty as humans to love one another and take care of the Earth. God created you as a spiritual body first and you must remember that the heart does not see race, sexual orientation, religion, or anything else that people tend to judge each other by! Everyone should have the opportunity of experiencing the greatest gift of all...LOVE. This is why charity should be an important part of all our lives because a small amount of care and concern can go a long way in a person's life. There are all sorts of ways you can volunteer your time to show your love for humanity and promote harmony. You can get involved with a mentoring program, volunteer at a soup kitchen, or participate in a community cleanup project. When you spread love and become a great giver, you also become a great receiver.

The important thing to remember about spreading love is that it's easy to do because it costs you nothing. Always humble yourself and help those in need if you are able. You never know what a person is going through or what a person has been through. One of the cardinal rules that I was taught growing up was that you should never judge a book by its cover. I always kept this in mind as I was growing up in poverty and it caused me to hold my head up high and walk with confidence. I did this because I never wanted anyone to look down on me or my family because of our financial situation. It caused me to become a champion for the little guys/gals, misfits, and underdogs of the world, which I still favor today in my quest to be a better individual. In order to escape poverty and never return to poverty, you have to show compassion and empathy to your fellow man because the tables can always turn

in life.

Chess Move #11: Pay it forward today! Do something nice for someone you don't know. Whether it's paying for their groceries or buying someone a cup of coffee. It will come back to you 10 fold when your heart is sincere.

FIND YOUR SOUL MATE

"I'd rather be in love because two incomes go much further than one"

Remember the 80's movie weird science? It's the one where the two geeky guys (Gary & Wyatt) create the girl of every man's dream! Once everyone finds out that the beautiful goddess of a woman is completely loyal to her creators, the two buddies' instantly become the life of the party. Only if things were that simple in real life, everyone would create the perfect mate using this machine. The truth is there's no such thing as the perfect mate. Everyone has their faults and weaknesses and it's unrealistic to think otherwise. It was easy for me to find my soul mate because she possessed the main quality that I've always looked for in women and that's intelligence. I realized at a very young age that the smart people are usually the hardest workers. When I met my wife I was intrigued at the fact that she had four different jobs. It was a match made in heaven for us but it made me realize that there's someone for everybody.

If you're single, don't give up on love because the right person is being prepared for you it's just a matter of time before you cross paths. If you are going to travel the murky waters of life, it seems to be much more difficult to do alone. When you have a soul mate it makes it easier to escape from poverty because two incomes can have more impact than one. You have to be able to get past all of your personal insecurities in order to make room for love. Finding your soul mate is a lot of hard work because it requires you to apply yourself in many different areas of life. Many people say that you should sit back and wait for love to find you but what if that never happens? If you do these three things you will give yourself a better chance of finding your soul mate and winning at life.

1. Be Confident

People can sense when a person lacks confidence and this is a complete turn-off! Be conscious of how you interact with the world around you because too much of anything is bad for you. If you come across as being too confident it can easily be interpreted as arrogance and cockiness. I've learned that there's a thin line between the two. The key is to always be humble and courteous. If you have good manners people will always be kind to you and if you couple this with confidence, you'll easily gain respect.

2. Be Assertive

You need to speak with definiteness of purpose and be clear about your goals in life. Assertiveness deals with the manner in which you communicate and you must pick your words carefully. The key is to always be direct and straight forward but do it in a nice way. You don't want to come across as aggressive so be sure to watch the tone and speed of your voice. People just need to know that you mean business when you discuss anything of interest to you.

3. Be Yourself

It's extremely important for you to be comfortable in your own skin at all times! Anyone that knows you should be able to use the same words to describe you. If a person doesn't like you the way you are, it should let you know that they don't really like you at all. True beauty is on the inside and no matter what your physical appearance consists of, it's not who you really are. You are really the spirit inside and the mind that creates the personality that interacts with people. Everyone in the world is different and we all have unique qualities that we bring to the table. Finding your soul mate won't help you fill certain voids if you haven't done the work on yourself first.

Now that the three-step process has been laid out it's time to go to the lab like Gary and Wyatt to start working on the masterpiece! The good thing is that your machine works a lot better than the one these guys used back in the 80's film because your machine is your mind. Always remember that thoughts become things and you must first create the image of your soul mate in your mind. Once you have done this it's time to focus on the three things outlined above. Lastly, the universe is going to respond to your thoughts and actions and send you the soul mate of your dreams. You are now required to love and respect your soul mate as you build a winning future together.

Chess Move #12: Whether you are single or in a relationship, give out 5 compliments today. Not only will this help you improve your confidence but it will make someone else feel better about them. Giving compliments also allows you to become more comfortable with receiving compliments.

COMMUNICATION IS KEY

"A closed mouth does not get fed"

Today is your birthday and you are literally 30 seconds old. You can hear the sound of machines beeping, people murmuring, and there's a combination of laughter and crying as you struggle to open your eyes. You can feel yourself floating in the air being passed around as your umbilical cord is being cut and you are handed to your mother for the very first time. There's just so much confusion going on around you and you just don't know what to do except for cry. You begin to let out this low-pitch cry that sounds like a small broken siren that will not shut off. You finally calm down because you can hear your mother's voice and you recall the rhythm of your mother's heartbeat as you lay on her chest while being caressed. I'm probably far from correct on the way your childbirth went down but if I had to imagine my own it would be similar to that depiction. I said all that to say that the moment you entered the world you began to communicate. You had to listen and pay attention to the things going on around you and once that was done, you let everyone know how it felt to be outside the warm comfort of your mother's womb and be in a cold noisy room with people passing you around.

Therefore, it's from this day and for the rest of your life that you will have engaged in some form of communication unless you are physically or psychologically unable to do so. Communication is going to be an important weapon as you battle the vicious beast called poverty. Just think about it, everything you do in life requires you to communicate! Whether you're speaking to your friend about last night's basketball game, reading a book on your kindle, listening to a song on your iPod, or trying to make sense of a crazy news story as you watch TV, it all requires communication. If you master the art of communication you triple your chances of having major success when it comes to love, career, finances, and self-confidence.

The main thing that we must all remember is that what you say and how you say it is very important. Later in life I learned the breakdown on how communication really works. To take this point even further, I was shocked to learn that communication is largely based on what you do not say. What I mean by this is: 55% of communication is nonverbal, 38% is tone of voice, and only 7% is verbal (what you say). Let's assume your name is

Taylor and I were to ask you, "Taylor do you want to go to the mall with me?" and after hearing me ask this question, you turn around with your nose in the air and a stank look on your face and say in a dull muffled tone, "Yeah, I'll go to the mall with you". Even though you agreed to go to the mall with me doesn't mean you really wanted to go with me. The way you looked and how you sounded when answering my question gave it all away, you didn't really want to go! You always have to be conscious of what you are not saying and how you are reacting to people nonverbally. A wise man once said to me, "See with your ears and listen with your eyes" and those words have always stuck with me as they should for you as if you are going to escape from poverty.

Chess Move #13: Exercise controlling your body language today. Make sure that you are communicating effectively when you are not speaking. Always remember that it's what you don't say that communicates the most.

MENDING FENCES

"Holding a grudge is a lot harder than letting go of one"

It didn't take a therapist or counselor for me to realize that I was holding on to some deep emotional trauma from my childhood. When I was around 25 years old I had a Eureka moment and it hit me like a ton of bricks! I had finally realized that I was just dealing with bottled up hatred for one person and that person was my father. I felt like my father was solely responsible for our living conditions and that he could have done more to up lift our family out of poverty. It was also around the age of 25 when I realized that I was responsible for getting myself out of poverty. I realized that there were questions about my father's life, grandfather's life, and my own life that were still left unanswered. I knew that I had to get past this feeling of hatred for my father if I was going to ever call myself a man of God and be the head of my own household one day.

Around this same time, my father was diagnosed with prostate cancer which was a devastating reminder that life is too short and it was time for me to start repairing our relationship. It was so rejuvenating for me to spend time talking with my father during his final years of life. I was lucky enough to talk with him almost every day for about 7 years straight which changed my outlook on life because I learned so much. The best thing I learned was that holding grudges is not the way to happiness. The person that ends up getting hurt the most is you and if you are going to be successful and win at life, you must let go of any grudges against those who have wronged you. Always remember that forgiveness is not for the other person, forgiveness is for you!

Chess Move #14: Forgive someone today. Don't live your life holding on to old baggage. It's like having a bad tooth in your mouth, you know it has to come out and if you leave it there it will cause decay and potentially heart problems.

BUILD BETTER RELATIONSHIPS

"If you want better relationships, become a better person"

When a child is born into this world, that child has no control over the environment that they are subjected to. This means that the child has no control over the people that they are exposed to and it's the parent or guardian's role to make sure that the child is in a safe environment at all times. Can you imagine being an adult and having no control over the environment or the people that you are exposed to? It didn't take me long to realize it but poverty forced me into a vicious cycle of bad relationships. I know that no one is perfect and that there is no such thing as the perfect relationship, so I can't speak for everyone that grew up in a poverty stricken environment but I learned at a very early age that there are people out there that don't want to hear you talk about positive news. These same people don't want to hear about your personal achievements and they hate to see you smiling and happy on a consistent basis. This is sad but it happens all the time because some people are so dissatisfied with their own personal situations and find comfort in the discomfort of others; it's the old crabs in the bucket mentality. Another sad part is that, it's usually the people closest to you that tend to hurt you most such as family members, longtime friends, and co-workers.

As for my family, it was like a contest to see whose life situation was worse and if it happened to be yours, you were the topic of discussion amongst the entire family. Now don't get me wrong, not everyone in my family is this way and I'm not saying for you to go out and get a new family. I'm stressing this because I come from a huge family and I've been submerged in the good and bad side of black culture in America and family was the easiest for me to study as I began examining culture and relationships. Besides that, my mother and father were the black sheep of their families and we had no money and they fought constantly. There was always some off the wall story involving my parents that everyone else found entertaining, yet I found embarrassing so I came up with a strategy to deal with all my relatives. The plan I devised was to become the best son, grandson, brother, cousin, and nephew that I could possibly be. If people were going to say anything about me, I made sure that it was going to be something nice. I was the poster child for "Yes ma'am" and "No ma'am" growing up. All the adults knew that I was respectful and well behaved.

Whenever I was around my cousins, I made sure that they were all having fun and enjoying themselves, which meant I had to be extra creative, charismatic, and funny. This worked out well for me because I still have great relationships with all my family members.

As for friends and co-workers, it's much easier to find new friends and co-workers than it is to find new family members. You should always keep yourself around positive people that are going to help you grow. You never want to get stuck with a group of people that are stagnant in life and complain all the time. You definitely don't want to be around people that gossip all the time even if they are talking about the latest reality TV scoop. One of my favorite anonymous quotes goes like this, "If you are the smartest person in the room, you need to find a new room." It's important to have stimulating and thought provoking questions on a daily basis. This type relationship will only cause you to be more productive in your daily life. It's all about stepping outside your comfort zone if you want to see better relationship results. I know this is easier said than done, especially for me because I've always been an extrovert. Some people find it very difficult to make friends with strangers or to stand out at a networking event. I wrote a blog article years ago called "When you're Interested People Will Find You Interesting" and in the article I talk about how most people are so focused on making a good impression on others that they tend to over talk about themselves. In the article, I challenge the reader to listen and be interested in the other person's story before offering up their own and by doing this you will have the person's undivided attention as you work to build the relationship.

Chess Move #15: Attend or enroll in a professional networking event today. There are all different types of events listed on Facebook and Eventbrite that take place each day of the week. Make it a point to step outside your shell and attend a function that will place you around like minded individuals.

UNDERSTANDING PERCEPTION

"Understanding your environment will always give you a better understanding of self"

Have you ever stopped and asked yourself how your environment has influenced the way that you perceive the world around you? First of all, you must ask, what is perception to me? Well, I performed a Google search of the word perception and the first thing that popped up was; perception is the ability to see, hear, or become aware of something through the senses. I totally agree with this definition of the word but if you and I were to look at the same abstract image, it would spell out something completely different to the both of us. Each individual is entitled to their own way of thinking. We all have a mind that was specifically tailored to each of us. This mind is tailored by the environment a person is exposed to throughout the different stages of life.

The two main distinctions of perception that I am focused on in this article are positive images and negative images, however professionals in the field of psychology can surely provide research and data to show many other variations of perception. The distinction of perception that I feel garners the most attention as it relates to your environment is the positive image. We usually attribute a positive image to things that we find attractive or that we think might make us feel better about ourselves. Also, when we see things that are familiar in our environment, we tend to accept it as being positive. For instance, if you were flipping through the television channels, you would probably bypass the shows that you have never watched. This is largely due to the fact that unattractive and unfamiliar things may imply a negative image to you. These images of both positive and negative relate directly to your environment because we are all products of our environment. Another example would be, if you were to sleep over at a friend's house where it is unsanitary. You would probably feel uncomfortable and would certainly not sleep as well as you would in a clean home. Environment is a major factor because it can affect whether you have a positive or negative image to apply to a person, place, or thing.

In addition to your environment, the media also plays a major role in determining how we think and perceive things. Today, we live in a world that's largely driven by social media and we use blog sites and magazines to dictate images of beauty. If the so-called fashion experts that examine the red carpets at major celebrity galas don't call it glamorous or say it's out of season you don't think you have any style. Also, many of us won't own up to the fact that we are obsessed with reality TV. To make matters worse, you can't turn on the TV without seeing a headline story about the latest celebrity breakup or political scandal, as if there's no better news! Statistics and stereotypes have also trained us to think a certain way and I don't expect this to change much in the coming years. People today are more focused on material things than moral things and this could be why there are so many problems facing the world.

Usually, when a person grows up in a poverty stricken environment, they are exposed to more negative images than positive ones, which I can relate to. It is easy for a person to get distracted when you only see negative images in your environment and at the same time, the media is indirectly shaping your perception for you. This is especially a problem in the black community because black males are constantly seeking validation and are struggling to establish their identities in the professional world. This is why it's very important that everyone, no matter your race, take the time to start thinking for yourselves and reasoning with the challenges that are facing society. The only way to fix a problem of this magnitude is for people to come together and work together.

It shouldn't matter what type of environment you have been exposed to because everyone brings something unique to the table. People can come from a negative environment and not conform to the way others around them think. For some, the negativity becomes fuel and is turned into true grit and determination. That negative environment serves as inspiration, causing that person to be fearless and assertive in any environment. Understanding how people perceive you and how you perceive the world is an essential key to win and escape from poverty.

Chess Move #16: Ask a friend or acquaintance for their honest opinion about how they perceive you. Allow yourself to be completely inviting about their opinion. If you really want to improve your life you must be open to feedback. Don't be alarmed by what you find out. You must take the feedback and work on ways to improve everything about your life.

THE SIDE VIEW MIRROR

"You have to face the side view mirror at some point"

When I was a child in Chicago I remember playing a game called that's my car, some people call it bingo. It's a game you play while riding in the car admiring the other vehicles on the road and the first person that yells that's my car is the make believe owner. This game is the reason I'm fascinated with nice cars to this day. The game also helped me start visualizing the life that I wanted to live one day and if I was ever going to drive a nice car, I had to escape from poverty. The one thing about cars that fascinated me the most about cars was the writing on the side view mirrors; "Objects in the mirror are closer than they actually appear". This statement alone is very thought provoking and it makes you wonder about the person that coined the phrase. Did the government or auto manufactures go out and find a philosopher to write this phrase? I know it was just written to be a safety precaution for automobile manufacturers but the words have always resonated with me and you should apply them to your life as well.

Let's take a moment to break down the statement. The word object can be used to refer to anything such as life situations that have occurred in your past. The mirror itself offers a reflection and allows you to see what's happening behind the car. There is a mirror positioned at your left and right side which causes you to focus on what's happening next to you all while driving ahead. The driver has to look ahead and often glance at the rear view and side mirrors. The entire driving experience encompasses 360 degrees of focus and attention because your primary goal is to move forward and get to your destination.

Now let's focus on the side view mirror statement again; "Objects in the mirror are closer than they actually appear." I interpret this as implying that the past is more important than you think it is. The past gives you the personal identity that you have today. Everything you are is based on what has happened over the course of your life and how those experiences have shaped your mindset. The positioning of the side mirrors represent the present. When you look to the left and to the right, it's the same level that you are on being in the middle.

Looking to both sides allows you to self-evaluate. You should always have solid people around you and at the same token; you should be at a comfortable place in life based on the goals you've predetermined. Lastly, the future is represented by the driving experience as a whole. As you move forward in life, remember to be conscious of everything that's happening all around you and what's happened in the past impacts your life in a major way.

  You should never suppress your feelings about the past because it will only hurt you. Find a Life coach, a counselor, or a therapist to speak with about your issues. Talking to family and friends is okay but the key is to find someone with an unbiased opinion of you which will allow you to be completely honest about your feelings. If you're going to become comfortable in your own skin and achieve higher heights in life you have to take time to reflect. When you have been severely traumatized by past experiences it's easy to get stuck in life. It's like being in quick sand which makes it hard to plan out a positive future and set goals. As the old saying goes, "you have to face the music at some point" but I prefer the saying, "you have to face the side view mirror at some point."

Chess Move #17: Take some time to clean out your contact list today. There are some people listed in your contacts that just don't need to be there anymore. Let the past be the past and move on. If there are fences that need to be mended, you may want to take care of that first, however don't get distracted because certain doors that are closed should remain that way.

STOP MAKING EXCUSES

"Winners don't make excuses, they poke holes in them"

Have you ever made a promise that you couldn't keep? How did you feel when you realized that you broke your word? How did you react when you got called out for the broken promise? Whether the missed opportunity was intentional or unintentional, you have now damaged your credibility with whomever. The natural reaction should be to own up to the situation and never let it happen again. Instead, you will probably fall into the same category as most people and give a lame excuse as to why you couldn't fulfill the obligation. The fact of the matter is that excuses are like belly buttons, everyone has one!

The moment you stop making excuses and take ownership for your actions or lack thereof, you will see a positive shift happen in your life. People will respect you for being a person of good moral character. That's why everyone loves to deal with a straight shooter, which is a person that gives it to you exactly the way it is. A straight shooter is a person that demands respect because they communicate confidently and assertively without any smoke and mirrors. There's never any fluff or excess when you deal with a straight shooter because they don't give excuses. It's all about getting positive results and holding yourself accountable if you want to be considered a straight shooter. This type person doesn't live in poverty because they are at the top of the food chain. They are the CEOs, VPs, Department heads, and leaders of the world and this could be you if you stop making excuses.

When I meet a person that tells me that they struggle with getting the respect of others I always ask two questions: 1. Do you respect yourself? 2. Do you keep your word? Displaying self-respect is all about raising the bar for you. The key to becoming successful at self-respect and keeping your word is to look at yourself like a business. A business must do everything to protect its brand or no one wants the services they provide. It's the same way with people because you have a personal brand to uphold. If you're always making excuses you may as well be lying to people and I don't know many people that enjoy being lied to. The people that take ownership and avoid excuses are the top people in any area and the winners all hang out at the top.

Chess Move #18: The next time you find yourself preparing to give an excuse for something that you failed to do, use these exact words, "No Excuses, I will do better next time, my apologies."

SHUT UP & LISTEN

"You have two ears and one mouth for a reason."

You might have heard of the 80/20 rule before because there are several different variations of the rule, in fact there are too many to name. The one that I'm referring to though is related to listening and speaking. The 80/20 Rule is in effect when you are interacting with a person and you choose to do 80% of the listening and 20% of the talking. By doing this you are taking time to fully engage in what the other person is saying to you. In most cases we are so anxious to prove how smart we are or how amazing we are at something that we forget everything the other person has said to us. It's particularly embarrassing when you forget the other person's name shortly after they have just given it to you. The reason this happens is because we are so focused on asking our question or saying what we have to say about a topic that we completely disengage with the other person while focusing completely on ourselves. In order to escape poverty, it's critical that you learn how to tune out yourself when people are speaking with you.

It's also important to define hearing and listening because they are two completely different things. Imagine you had a bad day at work today. When you left the office someone cut you off in traffic and you almost slammed into the car in front of you. When you got to the grocery store to pick up dinner for the evening, a soccer mom in a Dodge Caravan whipped into the parking space that you are backing in to. After leaving the grocery store, you're now stuck in traffic on the expressway and your phone keeps ringing. You finally decide to answer the phone and it's an insurance rep telling you that you just inherited one million dollars and the check is in the mail. After hearing this, you scream "I'm not buying anything" and hang up the phone only to realize that the insurance company called from a private number and they are never going to call you back.

This is the perfect illustration of the difference between hearing and listening. There was so much noise going on in your head that you were in no position to listen to the person on the other end of the phone no matter what they said! Hearing is simply stimulating the auditory senses while listening is similar but goes a step further and requires you to process and analyze what you are hearing. I like the term effective listening because it requires you to listen with conviction and purpose. Effective listening requires you to be fully invested and mentally free of all noise as you engage in communication with the other person. You're not drifting off into outer space and thinking about what you're going to cook for dinner or what kind of perfume your friend has on as she tells you what happened at work today.

Chess Move #19: Practice your active listening skills today. This requires you to re-state everything you hear the other person say. When you actively listen you're communicating that you heard everything the other person said and more importantly, you understand what's been expressed.

PICK YOUR BATTLES

"Sometimes you have to live to fight another day, let's just hope there is another day"

Let's be honest some of us like to pick fights and are always in attack mode. Others easily go into defense mode, even when someone is trying to help you by sharing input on a specific matter pertaining to you. There will also be situations where the person in opposition of you, have no idea what they're talking about. In fact, I encounter this one all the time. I can easily tell when the person doesn't have a clue what they are talking about but I will just listen and let them carry on. I stand to gain nothing by winning an argument or debate with this person; therefore I will just leave it alone and let them bask in the satisfaction of winning a debate against me. I have no problem admitting when I'm wrong but it can be very difficult to bite your tongue when you know what you have to say is right.

The important thing to remember is that everyone is not always against you and that you are not always right. Sometimes you just have to listen and save your own opinion for the right time. If it's really worth the energy, the conversation and opportunity will present itself again. If it never comes up again, just let bygones be bygones and you live to fight another day. I know this is easier said than done but you must understand that timing is everything. If you just listen and master the art of timing, you will know when it's the right time to go to battle. What I've learned is the opportunity will always present itself if you give it enough time. The person in opposition to you will either come to you directly or be forced to deal with you on a one on one basis and this might be the opportunity you've been waiting for. If you're doing something that's noteworthy or gets people talking about you, it's only right that you are always ready to deal with the critics. The critics, also known as haters are mad at you because you are doing something that they wish they had enough courage to do. Always remember that you have two ears, two eyes, and one mouth for a reason and if you listen and watch more than you speak, you will escape from poverty.

Chess Move #20: The next time you get into a heated argument or a debate, take the high road. You don't always have to be right and you don't always have to win a fight. Sometimes you just need to let the other person say everything they have to say. You will be demonstrating self-control while the other person is blowing up. The next time you find yourself heading down a similar path, you will know exactly how to conduct yourself.

DON'T CONFORM

"If you go against the grain it means you know the definition of conformity"

When I was five years old we lived in one of the roughest housing projects on the Westside of Chicago called Henry Horner Homes. The housing project consisted of over 900 apartment units and each high rise building being 15 stories high on average. This housing project was notorious for being a center for prostitution, drug, and gang activity. It was obvious to me that our family was poor because we lived with my aunt and her six kids. My mother, sister, and I shared a room in my aunt's packed house. Even though we were poor, I don't remember feeling sad or depressed while living in what most would call the ghetto. I'm not sure if it was because I was too young to tell the difference between what having money and not having money felt like. I actually enjoyed living with my aunt because there was always someone to talk to or play with. I usually played with my cousins Latoya and Angie because they were around my age and we went to the same school. The school we attended was really close to the projects, it was called Dett. I attended this school with my cousins during the two years that we lived with my aunt. This was also my first two years in the public school system. I can remember going to school and seeing some kids act up and get into trouble. Some would even cause fights with other kids as groups of children would walk home from school. I knew it wasn't right to get into trouble at school so I made it a point to listen in class and be a good student. This is the earliest time in my life that I can recall where I had to make a decision to be different from everyone else and not conform.

We live in a world today where everyone does what the next person is doing and we look to others to set trends. Rarely do you see people go out on a limb and do something completely left field from what everyone else is doing. I guess it's because it's easier to follow the path that others have previously lain out rather than re-invent the wheel. I like to surround myself with trend setters and you should too! Let's take style for example, what is style? Do you have style? Are you fashionably loud or do you feel comfortable in your favorite pair jeans that you wear three times a week with the same dirty old sneakers that you've had for three years? To be honest no one else should matter when it comes to personal style because it's totally what you define it to be! If you want to put on a red hat, yellow shirt, green pants, and purple shoes and call it style then that's completely your choice. Many of us will plan out an outfit to wear in advance, check it out in the mirror, then ask someone around us, "How do I look?" and wait for the person to say "you look good" which is the wrong thing to do. You should have enough confidence to create your own style and not care about what anyone else says about your outfit because you are doing your own thing. The very definition of conformity is doing what you see everyone else doing and this is not a good way to escape from poverty, to truly escape you may want to create your own lane.

Chess Move #21: Don't be afraid to live out loud today. Push the limits and do something you've always wanted to do but have been too afraid of being judged.

LIGHT UP THE ROOM

"Enter each room like you have a date with destiny"

Have you ever paid close attention to how the President of the United States enters the room for the State of The Union Address? It doesn't matter if it's a president of the left or the right, the script stays the same. There is an announcement made by the United States Sergeant at Arms, everyone stands to their feet and the President begins to make his way to the podium. As he moves through the crowd the room seems to light up. The members of Congress all applaud and smile as the President gets closer to them. The people all want a piece of the president and some grow impatient as gives out handshakes, hugs, and kisses. I always look forward to hearing what the President will outline in the address because it tells you what direction the country is headed in from the President's viewpoint. My favorite part however, is always the beginning of the address because I get to people watch as the President gives a lesson in light up the room 101.

When you walk into a room you should light it up as if you were the President. As they say in the modeling and fashion world, you have to own the runway! The runway is everywhere that you set foot from your place of employment to the grocery store. There is always someone paying attention to you whether you own the room or not. People are constantly analyzing and evaluating you from head to toe. What better way to make friends and enemies at the same time than to light up a room. You must always remember to keep your friends close and your enemies even closer so it's important to make your rounds. You must start from the front of the room and work your way to the back of the room. As you do this, you are infecting people with your charm and grace and letting them know you are down to earth. There will be people that will find your energy intimidating and they will make a pathway as you approach. You should make it a point to engage them so that they find you non-threatening and let down their guard. Everyone in your presence should be comfortable with the energy you bring. There should be no strangers around you and when this happens you will be completely in your comfort zone and free to enjoy yourself.

When you look good, you feel good, and when you bring positive vibes to any setting, people will always want you around. There should be no subject off limits to you if someone wants to be entertained. Of course, you have to keep it classy, which reminds me that you should know when to move along. Whether it's changing the subject or changing the person, you can't allow yourself to get pulled into an unproductive conversation. You don't have to be loud, obnoxious, or vulgar to be the life of the party. All you have to do is make the people around you feel better about life and they will appreciate your energy. You should always transmit positive vibes wherever you go. People should be able to associate you with harmony and positivity because you have created a good reputation. Maya Angelou said it best, "I've learned that people will forget what you said, people will forget what you did, but people will never forget how you made them feel". If you plan to escape from poverty and win at life you have to start lighting up rooms and if you do it the right way, you're only a handshake away from success and happiness!

Chess Move #22: Go to the store today and buy a pack of name tag stickers. Next, write the word WINNER in all capital letters on each sticker. I want you to wear one of those name tag stickers every day for a week and notice how people react when you enter the room.

LEARN EVERY POSITION

"Doing whatever it takes requires you to learn every position."

Have you ever thought about how a small lizard like the chameleon is able to survive in places like the rain forest or the desert? The reason a small creature like the chameleon is able to survive in the wilderness is because it has mastered the skill of adaptability. I'm sure you've heard of someone being a jack of all trades and a master of none. What you want to do is become a master at everything if you want to escape from poverty forever! Everything you endeavor should be given the same level of effort and commitment. If you do this consistently you will see positive results in every aspect of your life from relationships to finances. If you apply this to a team environment, you'll sky rocket to success instantly! The idea is to become good at one thing then move on to the next thing and so on. It should become a way of life and a continuing cycle for you during the remainder of your life. This means that there will be no such thing as failing for you. If you don't accomplish something it's because you made the choice not to pursue whatever it is.

I'm not giving you an out because failure is never an option! I'm simply giving you cushion to change your mind because sometimes you are forced into making decisions based on circumstances. When you take the time to learn every position you are increasing the likely hood of success in any given situation. Your versatility will allow you to step in and compensate for the shortcomings in other areas whether it's people or processes. Learning every position allows you to become the super hero that always comes through in the clutch moments and saves the day. You will be able to fall into any role necessary to get the job done and when you're a person of this caliber, you're considered an asset!

Chess Move #23: Go to lunch with a new person at work today. Going to lunch with different people will not only open doors that you never knew existed, you will be forced to learn something new about your company. It's always good to learn about the people you work with, but steer clear of the gossip.

OUT-WORK EVERYONE

"Always do more when everyone choses to do less, it will increase your value"

The world is full of smart people with big fancy degrees and titles with multiple letters behind them. In fact, the world is over-flowing with people that possess raw talent, great looks, big bank accounts, and all the other qualities that many would argue propel you in life. Some are lucky enough to inherit money and status from loved ones that either worked hard or swindled their way into a stable financial foundation. Over the course of my professional career, I have learned that most people admire a hard worker. The ones that don't admire hard workers are the haters and they're really just fans in disguise! If you are willing to arrive early and stay late at the job, you are going to pull away from the pack. For one, you are going to see better results because you are gaining more experience on the job and we all know that experience is the best teacher.

Every task that you embark upon, you have to put your personal touch on it. This personal touch has to be so unique and distinct that everyone will know it was you because no one else puts your level of detail into things. You also have to be willing to go above and beyond and do the things that no one else wants to do. You must keep in mind that you won't be doing the grunt work for long, but you have to be willing to do it so that people know what you are capable of doing. Often time people feel like they are above doing certain jobs, even when it's a simple task that won't require much time or effort. Performing this low-level task might not warrant any financial gain but it may help you gain a favorable opinion from your peers or superiors. You want to be the person that's willing to do whatever it takes, as long as it doesn't force you to compromise on your ethics and moral values.

The best thing that you can do at the job is develop your own personal brand. Your brand has to be one that demands respect and admiration largely based off your work ethic and it must exemplify all the values that your company is founded on. It's also important to remember that you have to protect your professional brand, so this means avoiding negative people or negative situations that will lead to complications in the workplace. A true professional is able to predict a storm before it comes by always being prepared and ready. If you work hard on a consistent basis, maintain professionalism, and effectively communicate, you will create a positive personal brand that's sure to escape from poverty.

Chess Move #24: Go to work early and stay late today. It won't go unnoticed to the people around you. When people know you're dedicated, they will go the extra mile to show their commitment to you and always speak highly of your work ethic.

ASKING BETTER QUESTIONS

"Ask better questions and you'll get better outcomes"

Most people don't realize that knowing how to effectively ask questions is a skill that will help you escape from poverty. Some make the mistake of thinking that asking questions is a bad thing because they don't want to appear incompetent. However, not asking questions is the worst thing you can do personally and professionally. You've heard the saying, "A closed mouth doesn't get fed" and this especially applies when it comes to asking questions. If you never ask, you will never know. I've learned that people appreciate quality questions and they don't appreciate stupid questions. Some people will ask questions just to hear themselves talk. I can't tell you how many times I've been in business meetings or presentations and the speaker ends with "Any questions?" and there's dead silence before someone asks a silly question just to be recognized and get attention. Then, you have people that ask questions just because they are trying to be nosey and get information to gossip about which is very common these days.

One thing that you must remember about asking questions is that there is a thin line between curiosity and just plain old nosey. When you're curious about something, there's a sophisticated way of asking questions. Nosey people tend to pry into your personal business and make it a point to make you look bad if given the opportunity. You should be able to easily tell the difference based off the type of question a person asks you. If someone is genuinely curious about something they will set up the question totally different than a nosey person would. The question might sound like this for example, "I know that you like nice cars, what made you purchase a Mercedes? Do you see what happened here? The question started out with what the person already knows about you, and then ended with the question. A nosey person is going to set up the same question totally different and it might sound like this, "Where did you get the money to buy that nice Mercedes?" Even if the curious person is just being nosey, they took the time to give you a compliment at least but the facts hold more weight.

In business people appreciate good questions. If you're going to ask questions in a business environment, make sure you take the time to qualify your questions. By qualifying them you are asking yourself, does this question make sense? How will the solution impact my work? Will the question put anyone on the hot seat and make them uncomfortable? I've been in situations where people have asked questions to make themselves sound smart, yet they ended up on the hot seat. Asking effective questions is truly a skill and you have to be conscious of the environment when asking questions. If the question doesn't make sense to you, it probably won't make sense to anyone else. Remember to qualify your questions in your head before you open your mouth and you'll be sure to escape from poverty.

Chess Move #25: Don't suffer in silence because you're embarrassed to ask a question. If you want to get a specific answer, be sure to ask a specific question. Always remember, if the question doesn't make sense to you, it probably won't make sense to anyone else.

TURN OFF THE TV

"In order to deprogram your mind, you must turn off the TV"

When I was a child, I couldn't wait to get home from school and watch some television. I especially loved to watch TV on Saturday mornings because all the good cartoons came on before noon. My family usually had one TV in the entire house and I had to be the first one awake in order to claim the remote control. In our house, the first person with the remote control could watch whatever they wanted so I always rushed to beat my sister and brother out of bed. Now that I'm older I have a TV in almost every room and there's no more fighting over channels. In fact, I don't watch TV anymore, it usually watches me. For one, there's never anything good on the channels. Two, there's so many reality TV shows and they all do the same thing which is gossip, go to parties, and throw drinks at each other. In my mind, reality TV is the networks response to the internet. Think about it, everyone goes online to get entertainment now and with Netflix and other deals like this, television is a thing of the past. The last thing that made me turn off the TV is the FCC standards. It's like they can get away with saying and showing so much more these days. Even if you're watching a good wholesome family program pay attention to the commercials that come on in between. I've seen far too many inappropriate commercials that expose too much information, have excessive sexual connotation, or push the limits of gender and race. The next time you watch an animated movie with your child pay attention to all the adult humor and inappropriate content.

This is why I've decided to turn of the television and get back to the old methods of entertainment. By this I mean reading books, meditating, or outdoor activities like swimming or going for a walk. You should always take the time to educate yourself because learning should be a lifelong process. Be careful of what you tune into on television because many of the shows promote a fantasy life style that is not easy to attain or sustain. Get back to nature and enjoy the great outdoors. Don't stay cooped up in the house watching television and browsing the internet all day. You have to do things that will stimulate your mind and not damage your brain cells. If you don't turn off the TV, it will be easier to fall victim to poverty. Don't get me wrong I still watch some TV but I'm very conscious of what I watch because there is so much negative traffic. The next time you watch the news pay attention to how many positive stories there are compared to the negative ones. I bet my last dollar that the negative stories get much more airtime than the positive ones. The main point I'm making here is take the time to cultivate your mind and carefully monitor the information that you allow into your brain.

♛ **Chess Move #26:** Limit yourself to only one hour of television today if you must watch it. There are many productive things that you can substitute in the place of TV. You can read a good book, go for a walk, go running, work out at the gym, cook, draw, or go for a swim. The one thing you don't want to do is get sucked into the internet because web browsing can sometimes be just as unproductive as TV.

ASSETS AND LIABILITIES

"It takes money to make money"

My parent's didn't teach me the difference between assets and liabilities because they didn't know themselves. For my parents, it was all about surviving and for most people living in poverty it's the same. It's likened to animals in the wild; survival of the fittest is a way of life! The people that understand finances and how to make money grow for them understand the difference between assets and liabilities. The smart people know that assets are things that actually make money for you, it's not just possessions. Take my new home for example, even though my name is on the deed, if I don't pay the mortgage or fulfill my tax obligations it will get taken away. On the other hand, if I found renters to move in, then purchased a second home to live in, my home now becomes an asset. It's bringing in a totally new stream of income for me to enjoy however I choose.

Just like my parents, do you find yourself doing just enough to get by? Are you still trying to keep up with the Joneses and purchase liabilities that will only lose value over time? Everyone knows that cars depreciate in value the second you drive them off the lot but we still want to drive a nice car because it's all about the driving experience, right? I will tell you the truth; I'm guilty of all of this, which is why I constantly educate myself on finances and investments. You should do this too, so that when you get to a place of wealth, you will know what to invest your money in. If you take time to understand the importance of maintaining good credit and how to balance a check book, you'll give yourself a better chance to defeat poverty and pass down wealth to future generations.

Chess Move #27: Pay yourself first. If everyone else gets paid when you receive your paycheck, why shouldn't you? Always set a small portion aside for you before you pay all the bills and start wasting money on things you don't need.

GET PROMOTED

"Put the same level of passion into everything you do and you will never stagnate"

When it comes to the job market this day and age there are three principles that I have found to be true. If you understand these three principles you will be closer to making your escape from poverty and winning at life. In Corporate America, the game is to move up the food chain as high as you can go before its time to move on. You have the power to become a valuable asset to any team you're a part of if you master these principles. If you stay focused on your goals and work hard, multiple promotions will be in your future. The single thing that you can control is your own attitude and how you react to difficult situations in the work place. A true professional also knows how to carry themselves outside the workplace because what's done in the dark will always come to light!

Here are three principles to help you get promoted and win in the workplace:

1. You will never get paid what you are worth.

Most companies expect employees to do more with less. In other words, you have to always be flexible and willing to adjust to the needs of the business. According to the U.S. Department of Labor the minimum wage has been $7.25 since 2009, yet technology is changing faster than the blink of an eye. With that being said, companies are looking for individuals with a high caliber of skills and experience but don't always fork up the cash to employ these individuals. Sometimes you may feel that you are doing way more than what was outlined in the job description that initially caught your attention and this is why the focus should always be, *"Get in & Get promoted"*. Flexibility is a must in today's workforce and you have to understand this..."*What you won't do another employee will*"!

2. You must be coach-able.

I often find myself saying that customer service is dead! Is this truly the case? Or, are people unwilling to be coached? There's such a thing as constructive criticism in the work place but what I have found is that some people don't know how to effectively deliver their message to employees. I believe that every employee wants to be coached, from the intimidating-tough employee to the smarty-pants know-it-all employee. Everyone wants to know that they are valued at work and most people are open to receiving feedback on how they can improve. For management, the key to accomplishing this is establishing common ground with the employee and discovering their emotional triggers and personal boundaries.

3. If you lack emotional intelligence (EQ), you will never get promoted.

First of all, what is emotional intelligence? My definition of EQ is the ability to consistently display self-awareness and social awareness. You have to be conscious of how you react to difficult situations and monitor your own actions and emotions in order to be self-aware. When it comes to social awareness, you must take the time to understand your environment, know the audience, and truly empathize with the individuals that you interact with in the work-place. This is by far the most important of the three principles and if you take the time to increase your emotional intelligence, you can set your career on auto-pilot!

Chess Move #28: Repeat after me, "I've gotta make it to the top because it's too crowded at the bottom!" Don't spend your whole life listening to the dream killers, just win and be great today!

CONCLUSION

In case you haven't noticed this is not just a book about poverty. I like to call this book a self-help autobiography because I want you to use my story as inspiration. My goal for this book is to serve as a map that will guide you closer to love, happiness, freedom, prosperity, and tranquility! You cannot allow your fears over poverty to take control of your life! Don't let people, the media, statistics, or anything deter you away from achieving your dreams. There is so much hatred and negativity in the world today and you can't let these things serve as a distraction. Take the time to cultivate your mind! You have to create a plan for the rest of your life. As you embark upon the journey of self-improvement, beware the doubters and naysayers.

There is absolutely no time to waste on listening to gossip or he-said she-said. Make sure that you keep good influences around you at all times because success breeds envy and jealousy. Finding the love of your life is still possible if you're willing to put in the work, you will make more money than you've ever dreamed of. You get to choose the way you want your life story to end. Just like chess, everyone sets the board up the same way to start out but you should move the pieces around the way you see fit to do so. The chess pieces represent the decisions you make in life on a day to day basis. It all ties back your mindset and the way you view life. This book is designed to help you dedicate your life to personal development, social awareness, and economic improvement. If you take time and study the ideas outlined in this book you will be sharpening your tools needed to construct your escape plan. Remember, the main tool is your mind and if you keep God first, take the time to reprogram, and create a vision, success will follow. I thank you for sharing in my journey and taking time to focus on your personal development. I wish you the best of luck and may God bless you in all of your endeavors!

Please be sure to visit my website and follow me on social media!

www.Hawulife.com

NOTES

PREFACE
    1. "If you help enough other people get what they want, you will get what you want". Zig Ziglar

INTRODUCTION
    1. How to play chess, www.chess.com
    2. Poverty definition, www.merriam-webster.com
    3. DeNavas-Walt, C. & B.D. Proctor. (2014). Income and Poverty in the United States: 2013. U.S. Census Bureau
    4. G.M.Fisher, The Development of the Orshansky Poverty Thresholds (2003)
    5. US Department of Health and Human Services, Federal Register (2015). www.hhs.gov
    6. 2014 HHS Poverty Guidelines U.S. Department of Health & Human Services
    7. US Census Bureau, Income and Poverty in the United States: (2013)

REPROGRAM YOUR MIND
    1. Golden hour - Psychology of Achievement, Brian Tracy

CREATE VISION
    1. SMART Goals, Life Coach Institute of Orange County Manual

ACTIVATE FAITH
    1. Faith, https://en.wikipedia.org/wiki/Faith
    2. The Master Key to Success, Napoleon Hill
    3. King James Bible, Exodus 14:15: "Then the LORD said to Moses, "Why are you crying out to Me? Tell the sons of Israel to go forward."

TRUST YOUR INTUITION
    1. Intuition, https://en.wikipedia.org/wiki/Intuition

NOTES

    2. Edinburg Lectures on Mental Science, Thomas Troward

THE POWER OF POSITIVITY
    1. Hole in the donut concept, Napoleon Hill

EDUCATE YOURSELF
    1. Tabula Rasa, John Locke

SPREAD LOVE
    1. One Love song, Bob Marley (1977)

FIND YOUR SOUL MATE
    1. Weird Science movie, John Hughes (1985)

UNDERSTANDING PERCEPTION
    1. Perception, www.oxforddictionaries.com

SHUT UP & LISTEN
    1. 80/20 Rule of Communication, Life Coach Institute of Orange County Manual

GET PROMOTED
    1. Minimum wage statistics, US Department of Labor

Made in the USA
Middletown, DE
22 August 2015